BLOOMINGTON PUBLIC LIBRARY

205 E. OLIVE STREET

POST OFFICE BOX 3308

BLOOMINGTON, ILLINOIS 61701

DEMCO

HARRY S. TRUMAN
His Life on the Family Farms

Robert H. Ferrell

High Plains Publishing Company

B
Truman,
Har.

High Plains Publishing Company, Inc.
Post Office Box 1860
Worland, Wyoming 82401

Contents

Acknowledgments

It is a pleasure to express my appreciation to the Honorable Charles F. Brannan, the last surviving member of President Truman's cabinet, for his introduction to this book. Truman considered Charles Brannan, his Secretary of Agriculture, and Dean Acheson, his Secretary of State, the two best members of his cabinet. It was during his tenure as secretary that Mr. Brannan proposed a new farm bill, strongly championed by the president. If the bill had become law—it didn't—it might well have provided a stable, enduring, and mutually beneficial relationship between the American farmers and the federal government.

The dedicated staff of the Harry S. Truman Library deserves special mention. Benedict K. Zobrist, the director; George Curtis, the associate director; and the people who know where everything is located: Dennis E. Bilger, Ray Geselbracht, Niel M. Johnson, Philip D. Lagerquist, Erwin J. Mueller, Elizabeth Safly, and Pauline Testerman—all of them make it pleasant to work among the manuscripts, oral histories, and books about the thirty-third president of the United States.

Unlike conventional editors who so often only ask the author to "explain" or "improve," Alice Levine suggested alternatives that invariably were better than my original constructions.

John M. Hollingsworth drew the maps with his usual accuracy and superb skill.

And to Lila and Carolyn, once more my thanks.

R.H.F.

vii

Introduction

Charles F. Brannan
Secretary of Agriculture 1948–1953

From President Harry S. Truman's frequent public references to the farm and farming, it is abundantly clear that he had extensive farm experience. From his actions when he was president it is equally clear that he was dedicated to keeping American farm families prosperous and the nation's agricultural resources economically sound.

Robert Ferrell's perceptive examination of that background in this book provides the first opportunity to appraise the extent to which Truman's farm experience may have influenced his conduct throughout his public life.

The book draws extensively and with perception and candor on the president's letters to "Dear Bess," among many other sources, to describe President Truman's close involvement with the Young—later the Truman—farm. Truman was not a gentleman farmer like his predecessor, Franklin Roosevelt. Long hours and heavy labor characterized his experience. Simple farm duties gave him time to think, and working with the mules and other farm animals helped condition him for dealing with Congress.

But however much his early farm experiences instilled a thorough and sympathetic understanding of farm and rural life, the evidences of Truman's dedication to the welfare of the American farmer are indisputable and numerous.

Throughout the period that Truman was in the White

House, the Department of Agriculture's requests for funds with which to conduct its programs for supporting crop prices, although opposed by a few members of his administration and some in Congress, always had the president's full support. A unique procedure was used to make these funds available. The Treasury Department borrowed the funds from New York banks and then transferred them to the Agriculture Department's Commodity Credit Corporation, which operated the department's farm commodity price support program. The Treasury Department also paid the banks when its notes came due. Thus, the Agriculture Department was, in fact, indebted only to the Treasury Department. From time to time, for government accounting and budgetary purposes, it was necessary to cancel the entries on the Treasury Department's books that represented its advances to the Agriculture Department. This was accomplished by provisions in the appropriation bills submitted to Congress, authorizing cancellation of the Commodity Credit Corporation's indebtedness to the treasury. These provisions were also reflected in the president's budget, thus affording opponents a second opportunity to object. On each occasion the president's support was unwavering. Congress also always acquiesced. It should be noted that the interest rate paid by the treasury to the New York banks for Commodity Credit Corporation money seldom exceeded one percent per annum. The succeeding administration abandoned this procedure and went directly to the private banks, cutting out the treasury as its negotiator, and paid as much as five percent interest.

President Truman also understood that a healthy agricultural program was important to American consumers and that reasonable prices for food and fiber were dependent upon an abundance of supply. Hence, the department's efforts to maintain production of all essential food and fiber commodities at levels necessary to fulfill domestic demand plus additional supplies to help war-devastated and agriculturally deficient countries throughout the world had his full support.

A priority in that great international humanitarian program was formulating the Truman Doctrine, later supported by the Marshall Plan, that supplied food to the devastated nations following World War II and undertook to restore quickly their agricultural capabilities.

But perhaps the most convincing evidence of President Truman's dedication to the welfare of American agriculture and its farmers is the fact that with the president's full knowledge and approval, the price to the producer of agricultural commodities was maintained well above one hundred percent of parity—the measure of fair prices to producers—throughout his entire administration. Parity was allowed to decline in 1953 and never again reached the level of the Truman era; in the 1980s parity averaged around sixty percent.

American farmers never had a more supportive friend in the White House and this work helps us understand the reasons.

CHAPTER I

Early Years

As far as the eye could see, there were the fields and the horizon and the scudding clouds, chasing each other and making giant shadows across the fields . . .

Harry S. Truman, thirty-third president of the United States, never forgot that he came from the farm. He spent his early years on a succession of farms; after the turn of the century at the age of twenty-two he went back to the big farm of his grandmother, and from 1906 until 1917 he was a farmer in his own right. Then like so many Americans, he left farm life to serve in the U.S. Army; afterward in 1919 he opened his ill-fated haberdashery in Kansas City and in 1923 began a long career in politics. Through the years, until the end of his life in 1972—only a generation ago—he looked back to his experiences on the family farms. Some of this looking back, to be sure, arose from the nostalgia that we all indulge in as we get older. But much of it derived from Truman's belief that farming taught certain clear virtues and principles, that work on a farm reduced complexities, that out of the changing seasons and the growth of crops to maturity one learned much about the course of life itself. As a student of American politics Truman came to feel that farm virtues translated to political verities, that any success he achieved as a political leader traced back to instruction on the farm.

The memories of those farms in western Missouri were ineradicable, indelible. As the years passed and he spent his days in offices, first in the county courthouses in Independence and Kansas City where he was a county judge (that is, a county commissioner), then in the U.S. Senate, and eventually in his vice presidential and presidential offices in Washington, he would gaze out a window, perhaps, or close his eyes and think of his early years; in his mind's eye he would see the farms of earlier years. Missouri, like all states of the Middle West, had been laid out in square miles (sections) with so many miles in each township and the townships grouped in counties, in

3

accord with the plan stipulated in the Ordinance of 1785. Settlers went into Missouri in the generation before the Civil War and among them were Truman's forebears— people who were still living when he was a child and a young man. There they took up the square forties—forty-acre tracts that were a quarter mile on each side. The Homestead Act of 1862 allowed settlers four tracts: 160 acres. When Truman was a child, he could look across a succession of forties: some fields were first green with wheat and oats and later turned gold in early summer; others were full of corn waving in the wind, knee-high by the Fourth of July, and gold in the fall. As far as the eye could see, there were the fields and the horizon and the scudding clouds, chasing each other and making giant shadows across the fields as if someone were making shadow pictures.

At the time Truman was born in 1884, great changes were taking place that affected American farms. The rail-roads had reached into the trans-Mississippi West after the Civil War and were now able to take bulk grain and refrigerated meat to East Coast ports, where there was another development, far less noticed than the first. This development was the invention of the double-expansion, or compound, marine engine, followed by the triple-compound engine, which dramatically increased the available hold space in ocean steamers. Previously, three-fourths of hold space was taken up by engines; the new engines only occupied one-fourth the hold space. Steel construction now made possible ships of almost any size—far larger than sailing vessels that had been limited by the size of great timbers or scarfing. Although a process for making steel had been known for centuries, steel was difficult to make and therefore high priced. The introduction of the Kelly-Bessemer process for blowing impurities out of iron ore dramatically cheapened the price of steel and made it available for ships. The use of telegraph and, after the Civil War, cables provided faster communication and dissemination of grain and meat prices. These changes opened the produce of farms in the Middle West to world markets.[1]

More changes were to come. After Truman left the farm in 1917, agriculture also changed in many ways. When he was farming, the motive power was muscle power—that of horses, mules, and people. The use of tractors in large numbers in the 1920s brought an end to animal power. New machines, such as the self-binder and the combine, together with electricity brought by the New Deal's Rural Electrification Administration beginning in 1935, ended much of the need for human muscle power. Different ways of planting (the end, say, of checkrowed corn), the introduction of fertilizers and pesticides, new varieties of seed and new crops, like soybeans, the virtual disappearance—until the oat bran craze—of oats because there was no need now for so many horses and mules: All these changes occurred in the years after 1917. Family farms, basic units of production in Truman's farm years, continued but became much larger; superfluous farmhouses, barns, and outbuildings were torn down or rotted down. Agriculture gave way to agrobusiness.

In later years, however, Harry Truman dreamed of the time he knew and used the lessons he believed the family farms had taught.

Truman's Childhood

Harry S. Truman was born on May 8, 1884, in the farm village of Lamar, Missouri, 120 miles south of Kansas City. He received the diminutive "Harry" for his Uncle Harrison Young, and his middle initial was a compromise for the names of his paternal and maternal grandfathers,

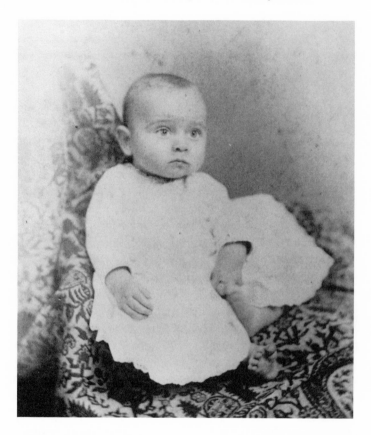

Harry S. Truman, 1884.

Anderson Shipp Truman and Solomon Young. When Harry Truman became famous, people sometimes asked whether he used a period after his middle initial. He usually put one in, but when he was in a hurry he left it out.

Truman's parents lived in a small, white, frame house, twenty by twenty-eight feet, that contained six rooms—four downstairs and two up. His father, John Anderson Truman, made a living as a trader of horses, mules, cows, pigs, and sheep, buying locally and selling horses and mules to nearby farmers; the other animals were sold to stockyards and slaughterhouses. The elder Truman conducted his animal business in a lot across the street from the house.[2]

Harry Truman was the first child of the Trumans to survive. A stillborn infant boy was buried in Lake Cemetery under a marker inscribed "Baby Truman Oct. 29, 1882." After Harry would come another son, John Vivian (known as Vivian), born in 1886, and a daughter, Mary Jane, born in 1889.

At the time of Harry Truman's birth, Lamar, named after President Mirabeau B. Lamar of the Republic of Texas, had a population of seven hundred: retired farmers and merchants who catered to the needs of farmers. It was a typical farm village. The *Lamar Democrat* did not mention Truman's birth. The paper, however, was full of ads, such as those for the Palace Barber Shop and Bath Room: "Shaving, hair cutting and shampooing with ease and celerity. Cleanliness is next to godliness with us. Satisfaction guaranteed or no charge." Cunningham's Drug Store offered the Papillon Skin Cure, "a specific cure for all skin diseases, salt rheum, erysipelas, rash, inordinate itching, ulcers, cuts, wounds, burns or scales and all scrofulous eruptions." The ad for Bird's ice cream parlor noted that it was neat, clean, and cosy, "and it is the very place to take your girl." Truman's father had an ad:

7

The house in Lamar, Missouri, where Harry Truman was born. The bay window was added after the Trumans moved away. Across the street was John Truman's animal business.

"Wanted, a few good mules and horses. Will pay highest cash prices for same. J. A. Truman, White barn near Missouri Pacific depot." One ad was downright lugubrious; Humphrey Brothers were advertising "Coffins and Undertakers' goods at 20 percent less than any house in Lamar. No charge for use of hearse in the city." In the local news items, the editor showed a bit of farm humor: "A. J. Cooper, one of the earnest Democrats of the county, called this week. He says he can't do without the *Democrat.*" And "Hoyt Humphrey has graduated in the

WORK MULES FOR SALE!

PARTIES WANTING TEAMS!

I HAVE

 HEAD!

OF

Work Mules

Well broke and well matched, in good condition. If you want a  TEAM, go to the White Barn, on Kentucky Ave., near Missouri Pacific Depot, see my stock and get prices.

J. A. TRUMAN

embalming business and received his diploma. Hoyt is thorough in anything he undertakes."[3]

The Trumans left Lamar in 1885, the year after Harry Truman was born, and lived for a short while on a farm near Harrisonville; they then moved to the seventy-one-acre Dye farm four and one-half miles southeast of Belton, near Peculiar, the well-known Missouri place name. On the first farm the father reestablished the animal business. On the Dye farm he took to raising corn.

Belton must not have meant much more to Truman's father than a place to buy supplies or sell corn. He probably did not know that Carry Nation, the crusader against the Demon Rum, who for a while changed life across the country, once lived nearby. Carry was a hell raiser whose husband—an unsuccessful preacher—finally sued for divorce. "David was too slow for me," she said. Mrs. Nation was buried in the town cemetery in 1911. Belton also became the burial place of another famous American—Dale Carnegie, who taught millions how to win friends and influence people.

After a year on the Dye farm, the Trumans moved—perhaps with relief, for seventy-one acres were barely enough for survival in the Middle West of that time. The move in 1887 brought them to the Young farm, which belonged to Harry Truman's maternal grandparents; there they spent three years helping with the six hundred acres and another nearby farm of nine hundred or a thousand acres, which was also owned by Grandfather and Grandmother Young.[4]

Harry Truman spent his most impressionable years on the farm—from 1885 to 1890. In the latter year his parents decided to move to the town of Independence, east of Kansas City, so the three children could attend good schools. John Truman conducted his animal business from lots next to the houses in which they lived until 1903 when they moved to Kansas City. Two years later the parents tried farming again near Clinton, and when a flood washed out their spring crop they retreated once again to the Young farm. The next year, 1906, Harry joined them and remained eleven years, assisting his father with farming and then, after his father's death in 1914, doing it himself.

What were the memories and impressions the president had of his early years on the family farms? His first memory was of chasing a frog around a puddle in the backyard of the Dye farm in 1885 or 1886. As he chased it he jumped up and down, laughing, and he remembered Grandmother Young watching and laughing at him. Another memory was of a joint venture with Grandfather Young—Truman must have been four or five years old for it occurred on the Young farm—that involved putting Vivian in a high chair and cutting off his long curls, an act that irritated his mother, although she said nothing to her father. Not long afterward, perhaps as evidence of divine retribution, Harry Truman, who was sitting on the edge of a chair in front of the mirror to comb his hair, fell off backwards and broke his collarbone. In the same room a few months later he was eating a peach and swallowed the seed, which lodged halfway down his throat. He almost choked to death until his mother pushed the seed down with her finger.[5]

Some early farm memories related to pets. Harry had an old Maltese gray cat named Bob, so-named because an inch of its tail was burned off; it had been asleep in front of the big fireplace in the dining room of the Young farm when a coal popped out and lit the end of its tail. The child never forgot the yowls as the cat ran up the corner of the room all the way to the ceiling. He had a little dog named Tandy because it was black and tan. One day the

Harry Truman (r.) and his brother Vivian, 1888.

boy was in the yard poking at toads with a stick; after a while he wandered away, following the dog down a corn row. Eventually he was discovered half a mile away, watching Bob and Tandy catch field mice. Someone had told Harry's mother he had wandered off and gotten lost, but she was unconcerned—she said that when the dog came back it would lead them to Harry.[6]

The Truman boys, Harry and Vivian, used to play in the south pasture of the Young farm, a lovely meadow sown in bluegrass. At the end of the pasture, Harry recalled ruefully years later, was a mudhole. The boys had a little red wagon that they took on their adventures in the pasture. One day they wound up at the mudhole with John Chancellor, a neighbor boy about their age, and Harry loaded Vivian and John into the wagon, hauled them into the mudhole, and upset the wagon. "What a spanking I received. I can feel it yet! Every stitch of clothes on all three of us had to be changed, scrubbed and dried, and so did we!"[7]

In addition to the games that the children played with each other, Truman recalled a few games taught to him by Uncle Harrison Young, who worked on Grandfather Young's farm. Uncle Harrison was a character who was hardly dedicated to farming, and more interested in expeditions to Kansas City where, as the nephew later described, his chief and favorite activity was to get three fingers around a small glass.[8] Harry loved to play games with his uncle who was a genius at checkers, chess, and poker (Truman learned the game from Harrison under the watchful eyes of his mother). He also learned pitch and cooncan, which are not much heard of today, and seven-up, which gave its name to a soft drink. Cooncan, from the Spanish *con quien*, or "with whom," is a game of strategy. Perhaps the world's oldest rummy game, it is played with a regular deck stripped of eights, nines, and tens; it is the

only form of rummy played before the turn of the century
that is still popular.

One of the future president's favorite stories of
childhood was of visiting a county fair at the age of five in
1889. Grandfather Young took him in a cart pulled by a
strawberry roan and drove six miles to the Cass County
Fair at Belton, and for all six days the two went to the fair
and sat gravely in the judges' stand when races were
called.[9]

It was during the year Harry attended the fair that his
mother discovered a problem pertaining to her older son.
The Trumans had gone to nearby Grandview to celebrate
the fourth of July; the climax of the occasion was a series
of rockets that exploded clusters of stars into the sky.
Harry jumped when each rocket blew up, but ignored the
showers of fizzing stars. He did not know they were there.
Before this, Mamma Truman had worried as mothers do,
for when she pointed out distant objects such as a buggy
coming down the road or a cow or horse at the end of the
pasture, her son had not seen them. Suddenly she knew
the reason. She probably imagined the most dire of
possibilities: Harry was going blind. In that period, many
families had blind children, and word spread of how life
had passed them by. A resolute individual, Mrs. Truman
did not tarry in seeking a solution. The family physician,
Dr. Charlie Lester, advised her to take Harry to an
ophthalmologist, Dr. Thompson, Lester's brother-in-law in
Kansas City. In those days children rarely went to
ophthalmologists, who usually treated old people. Harry's
mother was alone because her husband was away on a trip.
She hitched two horses to the farm wagon, put her boy up
on the seat beside her, and drove into Kansas City. There
she learned all was not lost, even though the boy did have
a problem. Dr. Thompson diagnosed "flat eyeballs,"
nearsightedness of an unusual sort, and prescribed a pair

of expensive, thick glasses. The doctor warned Harry not to engage in sports such as baseball or to participate in roughhousing because he might break his glasses. The prescription was essentially correct and remained almost unchanged through the many times Harry Truman thereafter was "fineprinted," as he described measurement of his eyes.[10]

The Truman children grew up immersed in farm life. They usually played by themselves because they did not live near other youngsters. Harry, the oldest, took care of the others. Mary Jane remembered how he combed her hair when she was a baby and sang as he rocked her to sleep.[11] The future president recalled the work of his mother, Grandmother Young, and Aunt Mary Martha (known as Aunt Mat), a spinster schoolteacher who spent much time with the family.[12] Farm women kept busy, especially in autumn when they dried peaches and buried apples. He remembered his mother and grandmother rendering lard and working over sausage. They used a recipe for lard that cause it to be "just as white as snow and to keep forever. They stored it in large tin cans and fixed some of the sausage," so he wrote a correspondent, "as you fixed it, in two jars you sent me, and then they would put the rest of it in sacks and smoke it with the hams and bacon. When I went back to the farm in 1906 we carried on the hog killing time just as our grandparents had done it but it is a lost art now." During his early years he became acquainted with farm animals. He watched the daily field work—plowing, sowing, harvesting, and threshing of wheat and oats; planting, cutting, and shocking of corn; mowing and stacking hay. Each evening at suppertime he heard his father—after the family moved to the Young farm—tell a dozen farmhands what to do and how to do it.[13]

Parents, Grandparents, and Relatives

The future president's relatives, his forebears, were all farm people or frontier people; life, in either case, was difficult because after the first weeks and months, during which they could live on what they brought, all settlers had to make a living by tilling the soil.

Truman's parents were interesting individuals, easily understandable in some ways—partaking of the directness of the Missouri scene—and yet complex in others. John Truman was born in 1851 and spent all his years in western Missouri, most of them on the farm. He was not touched by the great conflicts of the time; too young for the Civil War, he died in 1914 just as World War I began in Europe. Like most rural Americans in the days when farm labor was done by muscle power, he was a worker. He drove others as he did himself; the son remembered how his father pushed him, getting him out of bed and instructing him in chores from morning till night. There was no lolling around John Truman. Even so, the elder Truman was a gentle man with the family. Harry Truman could not recall his father ever laying hands on him; words sufficed. John Truman loved to sing and the family often spent time around the piano in evenings. Harry and Mary Jane remembered their father singing hymns in a light, pleasant voice.

John Truman was a small man. As a child he had been disturbingly small, even tiny. He stood five feet four, two inches shorter than his wife, and his granddaughter Margaret noticed that photographs of Mr. and Mrs. John Truman showed the wife sitting, the husband standing. Margaret thought it because of her grandfather's small stature, but, one suspects, that was the way Victorian photographers posed husbands and wives.[14]

Perhaps to make up for his small stature, John Truman displayed a considerable temper, although his irritabilities

16

Martha Ellen and John Truman, wedding picture, December 28, 1881.

rarely spilled over into family life. There was only one display President Truman could recall of his father's temper. He was accustomed as a child to ride on a Shetland pony behind his father's big horse; one day coming down the north road toward the house, he fell off and his father forced him to walk a half mile: If Harry could not stay on a pony at a walk, he deserved to walk. This incident may not have been evidence of irritability but simply an effort to teach a youngster how to stay in a saddle. But Mrs. Truman was not happy over the affair for the child cried all the way home. On other occasions there were unquestionable outbursts. A man named Rube Shrout appeared one day in an Independence livery stable to get his horse and buggy; he was almost in tears and a knot was bleeding on his face. He had gotten into an argument with John Truman who struck him with a whip. Truman, a dealer in farm animals, often carried a stub of a buggy whip.[15] Another story related to a court trial in Independence. An unfriendly attorney, a big, bluff man, was interrogating John Truman, and after asking a question and receiving an answer said, in an effort to change John's testimony, "Now, John, you know that's just a damn lie." John Truman jumped out of the witness chair and chased the big attorney out of the courthouse. John's reputation may have traveled with him, for a few years later when the Trumans were back on the Young farm, a neighborhood story had it that one hot summer day he and Vivian were riding together on a horse, Vivian in front holding the reins, galloping down a dirt road at a great rate. John Truman reportedly had a hatchet in hand and was on his way to settle a little trouble over a fence with a neighbor.[16]

The father possessed another notable quality: the willingness to take a chance. Where this trait came from is difficult to say. In livestock dealing he naturally took

18

chances as people were bound to deceive him. Such experiences probably had nothing to do with greater risk-taking, which may have derived from a vein of restlessness. The family often moved because John Truman was trying something new, such as a new farm. He seldom stayed in one place. He once acquired a farm that ran right up the side of a hill—near impossible ground—but he hoped it might be worthwhile and took his older son through a dozen creeks and forty miles to look it over. The two perhaps laughed when they discovered the lay of that awful land. John Truman was also an amateur inventor; he patented a reel for wire used in barbed-wire fences, and he invented a staple-puller for barbed wire. He also may have invented an automatic railroad switch, for which the Missouri Pacific Railroad (so his lawyer in those years, Olney Burrus, testified long afterward) offered $2,000 a year in royalties; on the basis of a dollar a switch, the railroad wanted 2,000 switches. The Chicago and Alton offered $2,500. Ever the chance-taker, John set a price of $2.00 a switch on the basis of 2,500—$5,000 a year. Both lines rejected his price. Later the Missouri Pacific used an improved version of the invention and John was unable to establish claim to it.[17]

In 1901 John Truman put everything he had, and everything his wife inherited, into grain futures after becoming acquainted with a high roller in Kansas City named William T. Kemper. Founder of one of the great banking and insurance fortunes in the United States, Kemper was a wily fellow, who possessed an instinct for investment and always multiplied his money. John Truman did not have the touch and lost everything. He was forced to move his family to Kansas City and take a job as night watchman in a grain elevator. The disastrous speculation prevented his older son from going to college, which the son wanted to do.

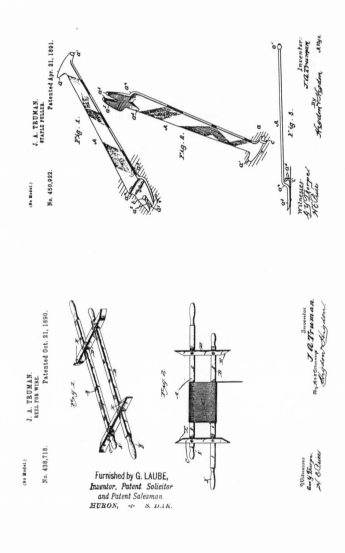

John Truman, an amateur inventor, held patents for his reel for wire and his staple-puller for barbed wire.

Some years after his return to the Young farm, while a part-time township road overseer, John Truman attempted to lift a huge boulder and developed a hernia that strangulated. After lingering for weeks and receiving indifferent medical attention, he died. His wife, Martha Ellen Truman, lived thirty-three more years (until 1947) and thus was much more important in her son's life. Mrs. Truman was a dark, pretty young woman upon her marriage in 1881 and a bent, gnarled old lady with a prominent, almost hawklike, nose when she died during her son's presidency. Her then-famous son was immensely fond of her.

The most notable trait of Harry Truman's mother was outspokenness. Martha Truman held opinions and did not mind voicing them. Her son, who was frank on occasion— sometimes when diplomacy dictated otherwise—must have learned from his mother. But even he believed she carried it too far. One time when he was presiding judge of Jackson County (that is, chairman of the county commissioners), he was tired and spent a few days on the farm, trying to get away from officeseekers. He heard his mother raking everyone, which got on his nerves, although he did not tell her.

Martha Truman always did what she wanted. In youth she had attended the Baptist Female College in Lexington, Missouri, where she studied music and art. The instruction may not have been at a high level; it was common in those days to denominate as colleges and universities small institutions that were little better than finishing schools. Still, it is possible that exposure to some of the finer things of life had made her something of a prima donna by the time she married a farmer and animal trader. She hated to cook and seldom did, save for her single culinary specialty: fried chicken. When her older son, his wife, and their daughter visited her house, they invariably ate fried chicken—or they were not well fed. Threshers never saw Mrs. Truman help in the dining room or kitchen—Mary Jane and Harry served the meals. She accomplished this near-miracle of farm life by refusing to do otherwise. In her first years of married life she cooked, but as soon as she could get kitchen help she did so; otherwise, she let Mary do the cooking. She never learned to milk a cow and once explained, "Papa told me that if I never learned, I'd never have to do it."[18] As she grew older and infirm, her daughter, who never married, remained with her; Mamma must have been a burden. Some of Mary's crotchets—taking her brother's car when his wife wanted it or burning letters her brother sent her—may have come from years of frustration from caring for her mother.

But there was no question about Mrs. John Truman's taking care of her children; she may have disdained some chores of rural life, but she drew the line at neglecting children. "If you get married, you ought to stay home and take care of your babies and the home," she said. She made the remark in old age, after World War II, when American mothers were deserting their homes and sometimes the children.

Mrs. Truman was always quotable. A lifelong Democrat, she did not understand how any reasonable person could be otherwise. Once a friend of her presidential son who was from Mississippi, George E. Allen, told her that he had not seen a Republican until he was fourteen. "George," was the quick answer, "you didn't miss much." When her son arranged a visit to Washington in 1945, she acted like the farm woman she was, even though by that time she was ninety-two and since 1940 had been living in a bungalow in Grandview. When she arrived by plane her son greeted her at the top of the ramp; she looked down at the crowd of reporters and the photographers holding up cameras.

22

"Oh, fiddlesticks," she said, "if I had known this I wouldn't have come!"

At the outset of her Washington stay, her son told her she would have to sleep in the Lincoln Room, presumably in the Great Emancipator's bed. An unreconstructed Rebel, whose father reluctantly had signed an oath of allegiance during the war, Mamma bridled at the idea. She told the president she would sleep on the floor.

Several of Harry Truman's more remote relatives were as interesting as his parents—such as his great-grandmother on his father's side, Nancy Drucilla Tyler Holmes, who was born in Kentucky in 1780. She married Jesse Holmes in 1803 and went to Missouri with her husband, who died in 1840. Thereafter she moved from house to house of her children, and wherever she went she carried her husband's tall beaver hat in its original box. Nancy Holmes's father had been a soldier in the Revolutionary War. His absences had left her mother with a household of children and slaves, and sometimes the mother had to defend them against the Indians. Once she drove the Indians from the door, only to have them try to come down the chimney; then she smoked them out by stuffing a featherbed in the fireplace. Nancy once was reportedly scalped and survived the ordeal by lying still. Although a photograph, taken in old age, shows her with a lace bonnet wrapped tightly around her head, in fact there was no truth to the story. Cousin Ethel Noland, the family genealogist, questioned her mother, Aunt Ella, who lived to the age of ninety-nine; Ella said that as a young girl, she had brushed the long beautiful hair of her grandmother.[19]

Nancy Holmes's maiden name of Tyler related to the family of President John Tyler. She and the nineteenth-century president were first cousins. Harry Truman thus was related to Tyler. When he became president, people reminded him of it, but he was not proud of the

23

Anderson Shipp Truman, Truman's paternal grandfather.

Nancy Tyler Holmes, Truman's paternal great-grandmother.

24

connection. He said his presidential ancestor had displayed no sense of proportion in dealing with Congress following the death of President William Henry Harrison in 1841. He might have added that in 1861 old John Tyler, living in Virginia, threw in his lot with the Confederacy; the twentieth-century president, despite his mother's convictions, possessed no fondness for the lost cause.

Truman remembered his Grandfather Anderson Truman quite well; he was a pleasant, slight, quiet old man who died in 1887. Grandfather Truman was one of those people who went through life without leaving much of an impression. Only one of his letters has survived, an ink-smudged missive of 1882 remarking the imminent birth of the stillborn "Baby Truman." A photograph shows the broad Truman forehead but a weak chin almost hidden by a scraggly beard. After marrying Nancy Tyler Holmes's daughter Mary Jane while resident in Kentucky, he worried about what he had done: Mary Jane had been visiting in Kentucky and her mother was out in Missouri; he had not asked permission to marry. To relieve his mind he saddled a horse, rode to Missouri, found his mother-in-law, begged forgiveness, received it, retraced his steps, and collected Mary Jane. In 1846 they moved to Missouri. Grandfather Truman's pre–Civil War politics were "the Union as it was"—that is, he was a Whig. He was a slaveholder. All his slaves were women. He inherited his human chattels from the Holmes family and never sold any. Mary Jane died in 1878, and Anderson lived on; he stayed with his son, and when John and Martha Ellen bought the house in Lamar they provided a room with a stove for the arthritic grandfather.[20] After the birth of his second grandson, he said many times that Harry Truman would be president of the United States. Harry's parents never believed this nonsense, nor probably did the grandfather. One of his grandson's early memories was of being in the room when the old man died. Harry Truman heard an aunt say sadly, "He's gone." The three-year-old ran to the bedside to pull at his grandfather's beard to awaken him.[21]

On the maternal side of the family stood a formidable set of grandparents whom young Harry knew far better than his paternal grandfather and who had much more to do with his upbringing. Like the Anderson Trumans, albeit two years earlier, Solomon and red-haired Harriet Louisa Young came from Kentucky, taking a steamer named the *Fanny Wheeling* from Louisville to St. Louis, changing to another that took them to Westport Landing in present-day Kansas City. After halting his wagon at the first portion of what was to become their great holding, Grandfather Young built a rail pen and threw brush over it, and grandmother stayed there—the rule for homesteading was that one had to stay so many nights and cook so many meals—while grandfather rode to Clinton and entered the sixty acres, paying $150 for all of them. Solomon eventually acquired large amounts of land, thousands of acres between the Big and Little Blue rivers on Blue Ridge in Missouri. He and Louisa worked together.

Another of Solomon Young's activities was to drive wagon trains to Salt Lake City and San Francisco. In the years before the Civil War he often set out on trips that lasted months and once stayed three years. Ordinarily he went west in early spring and returned next spring, with mule or cattle trains, six or eight yoke pulling two wagons, and if stuck then sixteen yoke on a wagon. Once he was gone so long that his daughter, Harry Truman's mother, who was then four or five years old, did not know him.[22] On one trip he reached Salt Lake City only to discover that goods he believed he had brought on consignment were not really sold. Solomon discussed his predicament

Solomon and Harriet Louisa Young, Truman's maternal grandparents.

with the Mormon leader, Brigham Young (no relation), who advised him to rent space on the main street, place his goods on display, and he, Brigham, would guarantee that Solomon lost no money, which proved the case.[23] During one of his trips the grandfather purchased an enormous tract in the vicinity of present-day Sacramento, or at least the grandson believed he had purchased it. The land was actually, Harry Truman said, in the name of an associate, who had gone bankrupt, and the grandfather bailed him out and took the land in part payment. Years afterward, at request of the then president of the United States, an investigation was made at Sacramento; no record was found of the nineteenth-century purchase. If it had happened, in whatever form, and Solomon Young had retained the baronial estate, he and his heirs, to innumerable generations, would have been rich.[24]

During Solomon's absences Grandmother Young kept house in Missouri; the responsibility was not merely strenuous but dangerous. One day in 1861 a Union irregular, James H. Lane, arrived with his men and forced Harriet Young to bake biscuits until her fingers blistered. The raiders killed all four hundred hogs, hacked off the hams and slung them across their saddles, set the barns on fire, and rode off. Ever afterward Grandmother Young and daughter Martha Ellen hated Northerners. During this visitation the family silver disappeared, and once when her son came home from a trip to Kansas, Mrs. John Truman inquired if he had seen his grandmother's silver.

Grandfather Young died in 1892. His wife survived until 1909, when she died at the age of ninety-one. She liked to talk about the past: She had lived in the house in Kentucky where Stephen Foster wrote his songs and knew him. In Missouri she had witnessed the great flood of 1844 and another flood of 1903, which she said was no bigger but there was so much more to destroy.[25] A few years later,

When the Trumans lived in Independence during the 1890s, Grandmother Young came to visit. In this photo she is sitting with Mary Jane Truman, Harry's sister, on the porch of the house at Waldo and River Boulevard in which the Trumans lived from 1896 to 1902. Behind the board fence in back, John Truman conducted his animal business.

wrinkled and gray, she posed for her photograph outside her farmhouse, sitting in a rocker, with Martha Ellen and Harry behind her. She represented the wealth and ways of older times.

CHAPTER II

J. A. Truman & Son, Farmers

"I have put about a hundred rings in half as many hogs' noses. You really haven't any idea what a soul-stirring job it is, especially on a day when the mud is knee deep and about the consistency of cake dough."

Harry S. Truman lived on farms from 1885 to 1890 and again from 1906 until 1917, and it was during this second period that he became a farmer. He and his father farmed together, until the latter's death, after which Harry continued on alone. The son was proud of the work the two of them did, and in 1914 arranged for a local printer to make up some stationery that read, in businesslike black letters at the top, "J. A. Truman & Son, Farmers."

His second period on the farm had begun because Grandmother Young needed steady help, which grandmother's son Harrison could not provide. The genial uncle was a big man who weighed 240 pounds, a large part of which hung around the waist. The son of a nearby farmer who knew him well remembered him as not much of a worker and described him as lazy. He assuredly was not a reliable man. He liked to go into Kansas City where, according to his nephew, he could purchase "firewater" and "rattle some chips." The uncle exasperated his nephew by getting into trouble in Kansas City and taking ill in the process; then it was the duty of the nephew to go to the city and bring him back to the farm for rest and recovery. Perhaps this behavior was a reaction to the dominating personality of Harrison's father, Solomon Young; it must not have been easy to grow to manhood around such a strong-willed pioneer. Still, regardless of the cause, Harrison was irresponsible, and the aging Grandmother Young called for the Truman family to return and take Harrison's place.

And so it was for only a short time that the Trumans, having lived in Independence a dozen years and then losing their money in grain futures and moving to Kansas City, remained in the metropolis. John and Martha Ellen left as soon as they could, early in 1905, exchanging a

Grandmother Harriet Louisa Young seated in the rocker; Mary Ellen and Harry behind her. Outside the Grandview house between 1906 and 1909.

house on Park Avenue for an eighty-acre farm near Clinton, Missouri. They and Mary Jane lived on Bodine Avenue in Clinton, and John Truman farmed by going out five miles to "the eighty." That spring he put in a field of corn, and a flood washed it away. In October they moved back to the Young farm. Vivian and Harry meanwhile were working in banks in Kansas City. Vivian immediately joined his parents on the farm, and Harry followed the next year.[1] Vivian, like Harry, had thought of being a banker, but unlike Harry displayed no aptitude for the work and seems to have quit with glee, for farming was something he liked—for years thereafter, he was a farmer, initially on the Young farm, and after he married Luella Campbell in 1911, on his own farm. Eventually he would

The only surviving photograph of Uncle Harrison, shown here with Mary Jane and Grandmother Young.

go back to the Young farm, by then known as the Truman farm, and he and two of his sons farmed it into the 1950s until most of it was sold and the land turned to other uses. In 1906 Harry may have gone out to the farm with considerable reluctance. It is impossible to say, for he never testified one way or the other. Friends predicted he would not stay longer than two days, two weeks, a month, a year at most; he liked to say afterward that he fooled them.[2]

The Young Farm

Between 1906 and 1917, the farm was an impressive place, and Harry Truman often spoke of it. Someone had named the nearby village Grandview because of the lay of the land, a high point from which one could gaze for miles in all directions—to the west for forty miles, all the way to Lawrence, Kansas. The Young farm lay between two rivers, the Big and Little Blue, not reaching either, on the ridge between, known as Blue Ridge, which extended down to Arkansas—a sort of little divide, as Ethel Noland described it, like the Great Divide in the Rocky Mountains. To the north the ridge shortly came to an end. The fall in the land from Grandview to Kansas City was so considerable that in Truman's youth the Kansas City Southern Railroad, which ran through the farm, kept a helper engine in Grandview, and whenever a large train came out of the city on its way to southern places the helper engine backed down to the metropolis and hooked the train.[3]

Acreage was large—six hundred acres meant fifteen square forties, a single forty short of a section.[4] Solomon Young and his wife had possessed much more land when the Trumans earlier had lived on their farm; upon his death his widow gave each of the seven children 160 acres. The farm that remained was big by Missouri standards, where farms of 80 acres were common and 160 considered unusual.

The entrance was impressively laid out, almost to show the size of the establishment. The farm lay along the county road next to a little cemetery, which Harry often described to visitors so they might identify the farm ("that is where you get off").[5] A visitor turned at right angles from the road, eastward up a long lane lined with four rows of big maples. Grandfather Young and Harry's mother had planted those trees after the Civil War.

During Grandfather Young's time a stately house had graced the end of the maple lane; the house was built in 1867 or 1868, but it burned a year after the grandfather's death. No photograph of this first house has survived. No one thought much about how it looked until Harry Truman became president. Truman remembered its colonial style. There was a small front porch, with a second-story door that led to the "portico," a deck on top of the porch. Windows all had green shutters. Inside a center hall opened on large rooms to each side. A stairway in the middle led to bedrooms upstairs. The house reached back on the east side to a large dining room, and behind it the kitchen. Under the kitchen was a cellar. Porches stretched along the north and south sides, and when Truman lived in the house as a child he made the north porch into a race track. The house looked like many houses of the Civil War era that can still be seen in the Middle West; some are made of brick, others of wood. The Young house was built of wood, according to Vivian, who once graphically related the cause of the terrible fire. A black servant ("a nigger wench," said the unabashed Vivian) was filling a lamp from a can of coal oil, and uncertain how much oil was in the can she lit a match to see.[6] Everything went, including records and furniture Solomon Young had brought on the steamboat from

Kentucky. The family Bible, with its listing of Young ancestors, burned.

In the next year, 1894, Grandmother Young replaced the destroyed house with a much smaller one, intending it as a tenant house. But she never built another big house. This new house, erected on the same foundation as its predecessor, was the place that to Harry Truman became so familiar. It similarly had two rooms in front, living room and parlor, in accord with custom of the time. Back of them was a smaller room, the dining room, and back of it a narrow kitchen. The latter had an outside screened porch, quite small compared to the porches of the burned house. Separating parlor and living room was a stairway that took residents to bedrooms over each. Harry Truman's mother and sister had the bedrooms. Behind them was a smaller room with sloped ceiling—Harry's bedroom. Like the little house of years earlier in Lamar, the Grandview farmhouse was not "modern"—there was no running water. Outside the porch, convenient to the kitchen, was a well with a wooden frame over it, wheel at the top, around which stretched the rope on which one pulled to raise the bucket below. The arrangement was workable if primitive. After a day in the field Harry Truman would take a bath in a tub of water that had been warming in the sun since morning.[7]

Next to the house, a couple of hundred feet away, was the barn, a slope-roof affair erected the same year as the first house. Forty-five by seventy feet, it was made out of huge walnut timbers taken from a mill built by Edward A. Hickman who had come to Jackson County a few years before Solomon Young. (The mill owner got into difficulties during the panic of 1857, went out of business, and the building was torn down.) The barn also used timbers from a washed-out bridge across the Blue River. George Kemper (no relation to the moneyed Kemper of

J. A. Truman & Son, Farmers

Mary Jane, whose album contained this photograph, captioned it "The barn that Grandpa built."

Kansas City) built the barn. Inside, on each side, were stalls for horses, mules, and cows. In front were the usual double doors that allowed room for bringing in a wagon and machinery. Over the top in front a peaked overhang housed a pulley to swing bales of hay or straw into the loft. The barn was as much a center of farm life as the house, and probably more so, as farmers spent more time there. On rainy days Harry Truman and his father and the hired men oiled harness or fixed machinery, and on good days they brought in what they needed for the stock or storage.

The Young farm looked like a big farm ought to look— even after the smaller house replaced the big house. The son of a neighbor liked to sit out on the back porch of his house during evenings and look at the Young farm and its pastureland, which to him was a beautiful sight.[8] In recent years two photographs have turned up of the Young farm in its heyday, when the Trumans were there before World War I. The photographs show rural beauty of a sort that one rarely sees now: a family farm that stretched out in

39

accord with the size of surrounding fields, a place of busyness, a place also that one could contemplate. The photograph that was taken in summer has the dull, cloudless sky that such turn-of-the-century pictures always have, but it gives evidence of the farm's sweeping proportions. The winter photo displays at once the loneliness, the isolation, and also the independence of the farm. No wonder that Harry Truman looked back on farm life, especially on the Young farm, as a seedtime for all his later achievements.

The Farmer at Work

A surprising amount of information is available concerning Harry Truman's life on the farm. Many farmers have failed to write down the stories of their lives, and their annals have disappeared into the dark corridors of history; but not the farm experiences of Truman. In 1983 archivists at the Truman Library opened a huge collection of letters beginning in 1910, which the then farmer wrote to Bess Wallace, later Mrs. Harry S. Truman, of nearby Independence. He and Bess married in 1919, and he continued to write long, handwritten letters for many years—whenever he and Bess were apart. The number of "Dear Bess" letters totaled 1,268. One fifth deal with the period of courtship. Many describe farm work in great detail; Truman told Bess everything he could think of. The letters are a treasure trove for anyone interested in what the farm meant to a future president of the United States.

Other resources come easily to mind for the life of Truman as a farmer. The future president had a habit of writing autobiographical accounts, and in the early weeks of 1945 when he was vice president and presiding over sessions of the Senate, he composed a 12,000-word handwritten memoir of his life. He again described the

Mary Jane at work. c. 1910.

farm years. After he became president he talked to groups of people in his office or elsewhere and made many speeches. In the talks and speeches he made references to the farm. Stenographers took down almost everything, which appeared in eight volumes of the series *Public Papers of the Presidents*, published by the Government Printing Office. The index for Truman's volumes contains dozens of citations to life on the farm. During his retirement years, 1953 onward, politics inspired more comments. His successor in the presidency, Dwight D. Eisenhower, had to deal with an era of increasing farm surpluses, which the government bought up under the price support laws. Secretary of Agriculture Ezra T. Benson stored the surpluses in huge rows of steel bins, highly visible in farming areas across the Middle West. Truman liked to comment about Republican farm policy. He talked about the old days and translated his conclusions to the new days; but no matter, the comments gave more details about his life on the farm.

And so the information, in wonderful detail, is easily available.[9] On farms at the turn of the century, as in all farm eras before and since, everything of course began with the plowing. The firm of J. A. Truman & Son, Farmers, first used a walking plow, but soon resorted to a gang plow made by the Emerson Plow Company, two twelve-inch moldboards on a three-wheeled frame. Pulled by four horses or mules, or two of each, it turned over a two-foot furrow. If a farmer could get an early start, he could break up five or six acres in a day—not an eight-hour day, Harry Truman liked to add, but a ten- or twelve-hour day. In spring when the weather was cool and he could keep teams moving longer without resting them, he needed less time. It was far more efficient than a walking plow. Moreover, riding a plow all day, day after day, gave opportunity to think. "I've settled all the ills of mankind in one way and another while riding along . . ." So he wrote while listening to the senators early in 1945.[10]

In the Dear Bess letters he described how once ground was ready, after plowing, he "put in" wheat, oats, and corn.[11] For the first two he used a twelve-disc drill that covered eight feet and had a marker on it so no skipped places would appear when wheat or oats came up. Once in

J. A. Truman & Son, Farmers

Harry Truman riding a one-row cultivator, c. 1910. Many years later the retired president identified this photo.

a while the wind blew, and in one of the letters he resorted to a little farm exaggeration. He told Bess that one day when putting in oats he had to tie himself to the drill to keep from being blown into the Missouri River. Every time an oat came out of the drill it went five miles before touching the ground.[12] Corn planting took equal attention. In those days farmers planted in hills and checkrowed them, each hill an exact number of inches from the next, so they could cultivate horizontally and vertically. Harry Truman's mother was proud of the way her son could lay out a corn row. She was supposed to have said he could plow as straight a furrow as any man in Jackson County, but she was speaking of his corn rows.[13]

Harvesting presented different problems. For wheat and oats it often was the unreliability of binders. They were an enormous improvement over cradles; no farmer wanted to return to cradles, as they meant back-breaking, slow work. Once the Trumans attempted to cradle a 160-acre field of wheat, probably because wind or rain had knocked down the stalks and the binder could not pick up the heads. Still, the machines were frequently cantankerous. "I have been working over an old binder," Truman wrote Bess in July 1912. "My hands and face and my clothes are as black as the ace of spades—blacker, because the ace has a white background. . . . I hate the job I have before me. If the machine goes well, it is well; if not, it is a word rhyming with well (?) literally . . . "[14]

Once when he had trouble with a binder Truman resorted to a friendly old blacksmith named George Plummer, who came out to the farm and followed the machine around a wheat field, a walk of a mile and a half, trying to get the tieing mechanism to work. The later president never forgot the result, although for the blacksmith it was a rueful experience. The day was hot, "102 degrees in the shade and no shade," and when he came to the starting corner he was, of course, thirsty. "He rushed to the corner shock of wheat and grabbed the first jug he came to. It contained lubricating oil instead of water. He took a long gulp and then he lost his lunch, dinner, breakfast, and the supper of the night before."[15]

Threshing in the old days was not at all like what it became after the invention of combines. In the village of Grandview a man named Leslie C. Hall owned several steam threshing machines and during threshing time took them from farm to farm. For each machine local farmers organized themselves into rings, working for each other, prorating the work if acreage varied. The system operated rather well, but had its problems, and Truman almost hated to see the great lumbering machine arrive at the farm. One time when the thresher came up the lane, his

44

On the right is Jane, the lady, perhaps Harry Truman's favorite horse; on the left is Jabe, one of her colts. circa 1910.

Mary Jane Truman with Grace Waggoner of Independence and son Denton, driving William the Buggy horse. circa 1910.

45

first thought was that, thank goodness, it was arriving after supper. Otherwise the Trumans (Harry and Mary, not their mother) would have had to feed all the ravenous visitors. They did have to put the threshers up for the night. As Harry described it, "We will have men and boys roosting from cellar to roof (we have no attic) and over the front yard too." Next day would come the threshing and the inevitable accidents:

Just as we get to going and the things begins to behave, why some pinhead with a young team will run into the belt and throw it or dislocate some of the innards of the thresher itself by backing into it. Both happened today. I didn't happen to be the pinhead either time. If that doesn't happen, some gink who is tired will throw a half-dozen bundles in the seemingly insatiable maw and choke her down. Then it's time for the owner to cuss and the engine to buck and snort. Any blockhead can choke a machine, but it takes a smart man to feed it all it'll eat and still go at a very rapid gait. I am not one of them . . .[16]

Harvesting corn was an almost equally complex task. Before getting the mechanical cutter into the field it was necessary to cut two rows by hand to make room for the horse and machine. Writing one evening Truman told Bess he had scratched his face badly doing this chore. He then tied skeleton shocks for the hired hands to fill, and a corn blade got in his eye; it did not hurt at first but soon began to smart. A blade, he wrote, was like a razor—men who shocked corn wore gloves and scarves.[17]

After this he shelled the corn, a dirty job. One Saturday he worked all day and "got my eyes so full of dust that I could almost scoop it out." Next day his eyes looked like those of a drunk. "It is a job invented by Satan himself. Dante sure left something from the tenth circle when he failed to say that the inhabitants of that dire place shucked shock corn."[18]

Hay, a crop that was not nearly as profitable as wheat, oats, and corn, was necessary to feed animals in winter and also to rest the land. Hay, like other crops, had its special difficulties. It required concentration and very hard work. To rake it Truman hitched his team behind the rake, not in front—an awkward arrangement. "If you desire to go to the right, it is necessary to make the left-hand horse move and the right one stand still. It works like the tiller on a boat—wrong end to. Sometimes you aim for a pile of hay and get one some distance away. I have arrived at the stage where I can generally go where I'm looking . . ."[19] Afterward came stacking, a devilish job. "You've no idea what a job it is to put up a stack unless you do it once." The first day his father permitted him to do it, the son calculated he walked thirty-five or forty miles around a stack thirty feet in diameter. It was necessary to keep tramping because if one did not, the stack would settle in an irregular manner and the hay spoil when water got inside. Nor was that all; after the first stack there were ten or twelve more, day after hot day.

The worst task with hay was loading bales into a railroad car. He believed it the hottest job of any on the farm or anywhere else, save that of shoveling coal for His Majesty—that is, the devil. He and one of the hired hands finally got 289 bales, he said, each weighing eighty-five pounds, into a car at 7:30 p.m.[20]

Harry Truman tried to do things on the farm the best way he could. In this regard it is clear that he was better than many farmers of his time who were content to mine the soil or follow other time-honored ways, showing little imagination. There was something about Truman that became thoroughly evident in later years, something that prompted him to do his best; he was unsatisfied with ordinary procedures if they produced ordinary results. His farm contemporaries noticed this. George Arington, who

47

lived on an adjoining place and whose sons were about Truman's age, said, "He spent every spare moment either readin' or figurin.'" He built the first derrick and swing in his section of the country for stacking hay. After he stacked the first cutting he sometimes covered it with boards for protection against the weather, and when the second cutting was ready he removed the covering and put the hay on top of the first cutting. The veterinarian Ed Young, who did Truman's animal work from 1912 to 1917, said, "Harry was always bustling around getting things done. I remember once when the Trumans were putting out a big corn crop, of seeing three corn planters running. A few days later I went by and was surprised to see the same three teams cultivating the corn before it was up. That was something new to me but it worked, as it gave Harry a head start on the weeds."[21]

It was said of him that he was one of the "weed-fightin'-est" farmers around; when he came into town and bought additional hoes, that meant he had rounded up some extra help to cut cockleburs and thistles. Twice a year he moved his fence rows, so he could rid them of weeds and waste.

Truman practiced careful rotation of crops. In a speech many years later he related that he had studied soil improvement and farm management. After sowing wheat on a field in September, he planted clover on the same field the next spring; when the wheat was ready in July, it was cut and shocked. In the fall he would cut a crop of stubble and clover. Next year he would have a fine crop of hay and also harvest a clover seed crop. He broke up the clover field in the fall and planted corn the next spring. When he had cut corn he used the stalk field as pasture all winter and then cut up the stalks and sowed oats; and then after a fall plowing, he would sow wheat again. It took five years to make the complete rotation—wheat, clover, corn, oats, wheat.[22]

Soon after moving to the farm, Truman and his father bought a manure spreader from a company in Waterloo, Iowa, and used it on the clover fields. Nearly every family in Grandview, a town of three hundred people, kept a cow or two and a horse, and the Trumans picked up manure from village barns and stables to spread on the clover.

The result of rotation and manure was a marked increase in crop yield. The proud farmer wrote that wheat went up from thirteen to nineteen bushels per acre, oats from eight to fifty, corn from thirty-five to seventy. In addition, the clover fields produced two excellent hay crops and at least one seed crop.[23]

A final aspect of Truman's farming that deserves mention is use of hired men. No single farmer, or two farmers, could have handled the six hundred acres of the Young farm. In those days of muscle power, hired hands were necessary. Field hands were both difficult and easy to find. Farm work was not as simple as it seemed; a good worker would be one who was experienced, who had worked for a good farmer, or had seen the results of poor work. It was not easy to find a good hand. However, many men could do the job fairly well under close supervision. When the economy was good, it was difficult to find help of any sort; in hard times, such as just before the outbreak of World War I in 1914, many men were available.

Hired men often lived in farm villages and were willing to go out on a daily basis and return home at night. They might have been artisans of sorts or individuals who found employment in the villages but could not make enough. In winters, of course, hired men had to rely on village work.

The Trumans varied the number of hands with the time of year. Usually only one or two worked day in and day out. Brownie P. Huber frequently stayed overnight, sleeping in the same room as Harry Truman. Boone (Boonie) McBroom apparently did not stay with the Trumans or work as many years as Brownie, who was with them from the spring of 1912 until 1917.[24] Other than Brownie and Boonie, all hands worked by the hour and day.

The Trumans treated their men well. The going wage was 10¢ an hour, $1 a day for ten hours, or $1.20 for twelve. But Harry Truman and his father always paid more—$1.50 or $2—and included meals. They felt better about paying such wages.[25]

Animals on the Farm

Teams of horses and mules pulled the wagons and machinery during the time Harry Truman was on the farm. In 1919, Missouri farms boasted more than one million horses and mules. The state's farmers were running only 7,200 light tractors, the sort the Trumans could have used; light tractors had not appeared until 1911, and for a while dealers sold only a few.[26]

In the era of horse and mule power, driving teams of either variety was about the same; the only difference was that horses were not as smart as mules—one had to watch horses to see that they did not eat while hot or drink too much water. Harry Truman remembered with affection the farm's mules—sixteen hands high, 1,500 or 1,600 pounds. They understood the rules about eating and drinking: "turn them loose in the lots where the corn is in full sight and the water's plenty and they won't drink too much and won't eat too much. They have really about, or maybe more, sense than a man who's trying to take care of them."[27] Mules, indeed, had many useful virtues. A joke seems to have circulated, when Missouri was being organized for farming, that farmers had a choice between employing mules or Swedes, and they chose mules because they were smarter than Swedes.

The principal problem with animal power is dealing with the different personalities of animals on a team. Truman was much bothered by the four horses he had to drive, for they were no team at all. He considered himself a horse psychologist, and yet it was all he could do to handle William, Samuel, Jane, and "X" (a bronco). William, known in the field as Bill, was an ex-buggy horse who hated work. His master found himself shouting at Bill in his sleep, hallooing, "Bill, Bill, go on!" Sometimes he was shouting the same message to Sam, a large ex-dray horse who never hurried unless poked with a stick or inspired by a bailing-wire whip. Jane, the lady, always behaved. Then there was the bronco, X, who always sought to arrive at the other end of the field in the shortest time.

It was necessary to feed the horses and mules, morning and night, a chore Truman's father left to the junior member of the firm, for John Truman usually did the milking. To do the feeding Harry had to get up every morning at five o'clock. He did not mind after he went outside, as for the most part—he wrote to Bess in November—it was not too cold; but he found it "awful" to start.[28]

Cows were attractive to farmers in western Missouri because they brought good prices in Kansas City. The metropolis doubled in population from 1900 to 1920, in the latter year reaching 235,000; Kansas City itself could consume a great deal of beef. Moreover, railroads had linked it to the East Coast where big, steel refrigerator ships could carry Missouri beef overseas. Cattle, together with pigs, were an economical way of disposing of the corn crop. In the Middle West of that time, less than one-fifth of the crop was shipped out of the county of origin. According to *Wallaces' Farmer* in 1913, 90 percent of the corn crop should never leave the farm on which it was

51

grown. A farmer was able to "condense" his freight charges by feeding cattle. Every steer could carry one hundred bushels.[29]

But apart from their ability to bring good prices and to carry corn, cows (so far as Truman was concerned) had a drawback—they were uninteresting animals, not at all like horses or mules. Cows, he wrote to Bess, lacked attractive personalities. And sometimes they were just plain malevolent. When it was possible to get them fodder without any trouble, they would not look at it. When it was hard to get, in winter, they developed insatiable appetites. "I guess I'll have to stay home tomorrow," Truman wrote, "and dig out a load of fodder for the benefit of a lot of beastly old cows." Their perversity appeared when one tried to milk them. One cow let Harry Truman milk her without any trouble. "She is the old standby and the old rip gives about a bushel at a milking." Her name was Nellie Bly, and he called her Purple after the classic poem by Gelett Burgess:

> I never saw a Purple Cow
> I never hope to see one;
> But I can tell you, anyhow,
> I'd rather see than be one.

Two others had to be milked after their calves obtained a share, and one had to have its feed in and be approached in a gentle and smiling mood: "Whoa, you nice cow. That's a nice cow." After the rope landed it was, "Now get away you blankety-blank speckled rip. Let's see you chase around the lot now."[30]

Cows almost became the bane of Harry Truman's existence. One day a man came to the house and wanted to buy a Truman cow for $42.50 and have the animal delivered at Grandview. Father and son spent a half hour chasing the cow and then decided to weigh it to see if the price was right. They attached it to the rear of a wagon and dragged it on the scales; it weighed 930 pounds and would bring $54 in Kansas City, and to the son's disgust John Truman decided that $10 was too much of a present for the buyer and turned the cow loose. It reminded Harry of Uncle Harrison's description of two yoke of cattle. One was named Episcopalian because it wouldn't eat at the proper time and tried to prevent the others from eating; another was named Catholic because it wanted all the food; another was Methodist, always battling; another Baptist because it wanted to run and jump into every hole of water. Harry said the cow his father turned loose was of the Catholic persuasion.[31]

Truman told Bess he was no gentleman farmer and if any cows got funny they would get a board instead of seeing his hat come off.[32] But that was easier said than done. In the spring of 1913 he was setting fence posts when a big malevolent calf, under direct order from "His Majesty," the devil, broke his leg. He had not been too diplomatic with this calf, had seized the tail of the 300-pound beast, "and made a wild grab for his ear in order to guide him around properly when he stuck his head between my legs, backed me into the center of the lot, and when I went to get off threw me over his head with a buck and a bawl and went off seemingly satisfied, I guess, for I didn't look."[33] For weeks Harry's leg was in a cast and he had to remain in bed or hobble around. During that time he contemplated the calf "gracing a platter," and John Truman did put a chain on the animal.

After Harry's accident Brownie Huber said the Truman place was hoodooed because people kept breaking their legs there.[34] John Truman had been bridling a mule, and the mule jerked a timber loose and broke his leg. A neighbor woman, Mrs. Hagney, was driving a buggy along the county road and when she came in front of the

Truman farm the horse turned over the buggy and broke her leg.

The Trumans raised Shorthorns and registered some of them. At the time John Truman died in 1914 they had begun to stock the farm with Black Angus. Mary Jane believed her brother sold them to pay the expenses connected with their father's death. One suspects he sold them just to get rid of them.[35]

The farm's pigs were certainly not Harry Truman's favorites. There was always something to do with or to them, such as putting rings in their noses.

I have been to the lot and put about a hundred rings in half as many hogs' noses. You really haven't any idea what a soul-stirring job it is, especially on a day when the mud is knee deep and about the consistency of cake dough. Every hog's voice is pitched in a different key and about time you get used to a squeal pitched in G minor that hog has to be loosed and the next one is in A-flat. This makes a violent discord and is very hard on the nerves of a high-strung person. It is very much harder on the hogs' nerves. We have a patent shoot (chute maybe) which takes Mr. Hog right behind the ears and he has to stand and let his nose be bejeweled to any extent the ringer sees fit. I don't like to do it, but when a nice bluegrass pasture is at stake I'd carve the whole hog tribe to small bits rather than see it ruined. Besides it only hurts them for about an hour and about one in every three loses his rings inside of a week and has to endure the agony over again.[36]

Like cows, pigs were perverse animals. A pig's head was always turned the wrong way; this was a hard and fast rule. One time Truman had to load twenty-nine pigs and managed to get fifteen into the barn. He then put corn in the barn to attract the others. All the rest went in except an "extra smart one," which grabbed an ear and ran out between Truman's legs before he could shut the door. He fell down, and all the pigs ran out.[37] When, however, the barn door was open and he did not want them in there, every pig would go right in.

Frequently hogs became ill from cholera, a dread disease that decimated—and in epidemic form could wipe out—the animals. For many years it ran rampant through the Middle West. As late as 1913, 10 percent of American hogs died from cholera; prior to about 1915 heavy losses from epidemics made it exceedingly speculative to raise hogs in large numbers. An epidemic struck Truman's hogs in 1912, and they began to die. He wrote Bess that his hogs had a perfect right to "kick the bucket," but ought to allow some packing house to do the honors. Of ninety hogs he managed to send thirteen to market and the rest took ill and died one after the other, until twelve remained. In accord with the law he had to burn or bury the carcasses within a given radius of the place of death. When the dozen had departed, he wrote, and he had performed "the last sad rites" over their burial, he hoped that as a result of his "dumping the whole works into one hole and one ceremony," the hog population would be zero. This experience, he believed, beat Mark Twain's prescription for the quickest way to pass from affluence to poverty. Twain had thought politics was the quickest, but Truman said it was hogs.[38]

For a quarter of a century veterinarians searched for the causative agent of hog cholera, but they did not find it until 1906 when U.S. Bureau of Animal Husbandry researchers at Ames, Iowa, came upon an effective serum. Truman had helped a neighbor vaccinate his hogs in 1912, shortly before Truman's died. Vaccinating pigs was hard work. Some pigs weighed 200 pounds and were as strong as mules.

It was necessary to sneak up and grab a hind leg, then hold on until someone else got another hold wherever he could, and then proceed to throw Mr. Hog and sit on him while he got what the Mo University says is good for him. A two-hundred-pound hog can almost jerk the ribs loose from your backbone when you get him by the hind leg. It is far and away the best exercise in the list. It beats Jack Johnson's whole training camp as a muscle toughener.[39]

For fifty years the vets and farmers thus vaccinated pigs until they tabulated the last case of hog cholera in August 1976. On January 3, 1978, they announced the United States "hog cholera free."[40]

At the time, hogs were worth the trouble, if—as Harry Truman said—Mr. Hog could survive hog diseases and turn into sausage.[41] Harry alone had the task of stuffing the sausage. Mamma Truman always wanted to do it, but when she did it made her sick. Mary Jane and Truman's father would not. Harry's hands blistered and toward the end he put blisters into the sacks, which he did not believe injured the flavor of the sausage. He got sausage in his hair, on his clothes, shoes, all over the kitchen floor; but it was worth it when the time came to eat sausage.

The Trumans and Aringtons argued over who raised better hogs. Harry had Hampshires, the Aringtons a heavier breed. Once Harry smiled and said, "All right, George, you raise the lard and I'll raise the meat."[42]

In the roster of farm animals, chickens hardly counted. Their only advantage on the Truman farm was that they were the principal ingredient in Mrs. Truman's culinary specialty. Problems with the Truman chickens seem never to have concerned Harry Truman, perhaps because there was essentially only one—lice—and Mamma Truman had the difficulty in hand. The lice problem came up in a letter from Bess, who kept chickens in back of her house in Independence. Her chickens were dying. This news brought a quick response: Harry gave Bess Mamma's recipe for chicken dip. The recipe must have been effective, for the lice would not have liked it. According to her son, Mrs. Truman took twist tobacco and steeped it in hot water as if she were making tea, with four twists to one bucket. She put in enough cold water to cover the hen and make the dip the right temperature. She added a tablespoonful of melted grease. She put her hand over the chicken's bill and eyes and "soused him good." Proclaiming the recipe, her son said, "Young and old alike can go through this process without harm." Harry advised Bess to pick a warm day. He also remarked (one could have expected as much in rural, negrophobic Missouri) that he would not fancy the job of dipping them and suggested, "Maybe you can force that negro you have working for you to do it."[43]

CHAPTER III

Beyond the Farm

"We spent a very pleasant forenoon and then went to the funeral."

American farms were lonely places at the beginning of the twentieth century, but the intense isolation was coming to an end. If time and money availed, opportunity to pursue interests beyond the farm was at hand. Farmers, of course, belonged to churches; fraternal orders, such as the Masons, attracted them; and farmers were naturally drawn to the Farm Bureau. Politics—usually small township offices—beckoned. Prior to widespread rural free delivery—if a post office was convenient—a farmer could send away for magazines and books. Harry Truman, who lived close to Kansas City, could attend concerts, musicals, and vaudeville at a time when the best artists, musicals, and theatricals, went on tour. A farmer could talk to friends and neighbors by telephone, the wondrous invention of Alexander Graham Bell, who first exhibited it at the Centennial Exposition in Philadelphia in 1876. Train travel was easily available and affordable. And during the years Truman was on the farm the automobile was "coming in." At first mechanically unreliable, it improved rapidly. More than anything else, the automobile changed the lives of American farmers.

It is curious that at the time isolation was naturally coming to an end, much national energy was being expended to bring it to an end. In 1908 President Theodore Roosevelt created a Country Life Commission composed of eight prominent Americans including Liberty Hyde Bailey, Jr., dean of the college of agriculture at Cornell University, and Henry C. Wallace, grandfather of the later vice president of the United States, and editor of the influential *Wallaces' Farmer* published in Iowa, and Walter Hines Page, the apostle of Southern living who was later ambassador to Great Britain.[1] The commissioners took testimony from farmers across the country through tens of thousands of questionnaires. They met with farmers in public hearings. They arranged for farmers to meet with each other on a day in December 1908. This effort was the grand business of assaying the quality of farm life. The commission brought in a report early in 1909. "The underlying problem," the report said, "is to develop and maintain on our farms a civilization in full harmony with the best American ideals." It suggested areas for improvement. President Roosevelt transmitted it to Congress with a fiery charge that repeated his injunctions about "race suicide"—farm women should increase and multiply the race or they were totally unworthy of consideration—but also urged the legislators to "satisfy the higher social and intellectual aspirations of country people."[2]

The Country Life Commission produced a lexicon of farm deprivations that kept reformers busy for two generations. It was not all idealism, for it did a great deal of good, especially when the New Deal of President Franklin D. Roosevelt resorted to rural roadbuilding and electricity in the 1930s. At the time, however, the forces of change were already moving in the direction the commission desired. Many farmers such as Harry Truman were already taking advantage of their opportunities.

Interests and Pursuits Beyond the Farm

The Trumans were churchgoers and like many Missouri farmers were Baptists. Between 1887 and 1890 they had belonged to the country church that stood next to the cemetery at the beginning of the lane that was the entrance to the Young farm. A Jackson County pioneer, Peter Thompson, had deeded the land for church and cemetery and was buried in a lot behind an iron fence in his own plot. In early years the church had housed Methodists as well as Baptists—it was a union church. The

Trumans' congregation, known as the Blue Ridge Missionary Baptists, seems to have been the group that annoyed Harry Truman's mother, who considered herself a "lightfoot Baptist." She believed the Blue Ridge Missionary Baptist Church was full of hypocrites. When the family moved to Independence in 1890, the Presbyterian minister happened along the sidewalk near the Truman house, saw the three little Truman children playing there, and invited them to Sunday School. Mamma Truman decided then to send the children to the Presbyterian church, and it was in Sunday School that six-year-old Harry Truman met Bessie Wallace, aged five. But Presbyterianism did not take for Harry, and in 1903 while working in Kansas City he was baptized in the Little Blue River and joined a Kansas City Baptist congregation. When he returned to the farm he placed his membership in the Grandview Baptist Church, where it remained for the rest of his long life.

The Grandview Baptist Church, the adult Harry Truman's church home, was actually the same group as the Blue Ridge Missionary Baptist Church, the "hypocrites" of Truman's childhood. The country congregation had moved to the village in 1891, renamed itself, and took the building along. The child happened to be out at the farm when the move occurred, and Uncle Harrison had something to say. "Come on," he told the nephew, "let's go see the old church walk off. It's going to Grandview." The village Baptists continued to use the country cemetery.

Exactly what the church did to lessen the future president's isolation on the farm is difficult to pinpoint; but it assuredly did something—if only provide a place where he could meet farm neighbors and villagers. In his letters Truman said nothing about church services in Grandview. He generally was reticent about his religious convictions. He may also not have met as many people,

Main Street, Grandview, c. 1910.

or as interesting people, as he did through other activities. Curiously the church's continued use of the cemetery provided in itself a considerable fellowship. Truman helped dig graves many times. He described one such occasion to Bess; it was not nearly as unpleasant as she might have thought. Six or seven gravediggers took turns working; the rest sat around and told the worker what to do, and otherwise retailed lies about the holes they had dug, the hogs they had raised. "We spent a very pleasant forenoon and then went to the funeral."[3] It was a Christian Science funeral, the first he had attended, and he found it impressive.

Next in importance to the Baptists in the life of Truman the farmer were the Masons, an organization that like the church held his interest throughout his life.[4] One day in December 1908 a cousin who lived on a farm east of the Trumans came over to look at livestock. He was wearing a jacket with an insignia displaying a square and compass and a big "C" in the center. Truman told him he was interested in joining the Masons. His father had not been a member, but had wanted to be. Both Truman's grandfathers were members—Grandfather Young in the

✐ Petition for Initiation ✐

To the Worshipful Master, Wardens and Brethren
∴ of ∴

Belton Lodge, No. 450
F. & A. M.

THE SUBSCRIBER, residing at Grand View Mo *and whose place of business is at* Grand View Mo *and being* 24 *years of age, and by occupation a* farmer *and having* applied for initiation *to* Belton *Lodge* 450 A. F. & A. M. *respectfully represents that, unbiased by friends and uninfluenced by mercenary motives, he freely and voluntarily offers himself as a candidate for the mysteries of Masonry, and that he is prompted to solicit this privilege by a favorable opinion of your ancient and honorable Fraternity, and a desire for knowledge and sincere wish to be serviceable to his fellow creatures, and should his petition be granted, he will cheerfully conform to all its established laws, usages and customs.*

Dated Dec 21ˢᵗ *A. L.* 5908

RECOMMENDED BY:
Wm. H. Waskom

SIGNED *Harry S. Truman*

The Petitbone Bros. Mfg. Co., Cincinnati, O., Lodge Supplies.

Harry Truman found Masonry fascinating. He applied for membership in December 1908.

Raytown lodge and Grandfather Truman in the Westport lodge. Vivian Truman would become a Mason. Shortly after his cousin had appeared in the barn lot, Truman applied for membership in the Belton lodge.

Harry Truman found Masonry fascinating. If he ever thought that membership might be of value to him politically, he never mentioned it. He received the entered apprentice degree on February 9, 1909, and next year became junior warden. He sought to organize a lodge in Grandview, and in the summer of 1911 obtained enough signers to start a lodge under dispensation. The grand lodge authorized a charter, and fellow members elected him the first master.

Truman the Mason soon was in demand among nearby village and town lodges, as he became adept at the ritual—through teaching it to the plow horses, he said. Lodges asked him to initiate members or assist in granting higher degrees. In 1924 the grand master of the state appointed him deputy for the district. In 1930 another grand master started him in the grand lodge line by appointment, and in 1940 he received election as grand master—a high honor. In 1945 he was given the thirty-third degree.

In addition to attendance at lodge he became the first patron of the Grandview chapter, Order of the Eastern Star, in 1913. Ruby Jane Hall of the threshing machine family remembered how he attended box socials to raise money for the Stars. She would tell him, she said, what box was hers; he would bid and sometimes have to pay quite dearly—as much as $4.[5]

Truman joined the Farm Bureau that same year. A county agent was appointed in March, and by the end of the year every township boasted a unit. In November Truman served as one of the committee members charged with showing people around the Washington

Truman mounted on a horse in his "Battery B" uniform at the Grandview farm when he was a member of the Missouri National Guard. c. 1907.

Township fair. "You'd think I was running for office," he wrote Bess, "if you'd see me chasing around shaking hands with people and displaying a classic cat grin."[6] He served as president of the township group and also as president of the Grandview Commercial Club; in that role, he helped plan the township fair he presided over with the cat grin.

On June 14, 1905 (Flag Day), when he was twenty-one, he joined a newly organized battery of field artillery of the Missouri National Guard. He remained for six years—two enlistments. His duties involved a biweekly drill. The men may not have drilled strenuously and any such exercise was trivial compared to "drills" Truman performed on the farm, but it was another way to obtain a little camaraderie. Guard friends, including one of the officers, Arthur J. Elliott, often came out to the farm on Sundays for chicken dinners. At one meal Elliott, a fat man, ate ten biscuits.

The youth may have enjoyed wearing a dress blue uniform with red stripes down the trouser legs and red piping on the cuffs and a red fourragère over the shoulder. While in Kansas City he foolishly wore it to the farm one weekend to show to Grandmother Young. "She looked me over and I knew I was going to catch it. She said, 'Harry, this is the first time since 1863 that a blue uniform has been in this house. Don't bring it here again.'"[7]

Battery members looked forward to summer encampments of a week or two in such places as Cape Girardeau on the Mississippi at the other end of the state, to which the battery traveled by day coach and steamboat. Another was at St. Joseph, where they camped in what Truman described as three feet of water on the fairgrounds. Lightning struck a tent, killing a man or two. This may have been the place where, before the lightning put a damper on the occasion, the men amused themselves digging holes in the flooded ground and enticing officers to slosh around and fall in the holes. At Fort Riley, Kansas, where Private Truman became a corporal, they fired real artillery pieces and obtained a taste of what lay in store in World War I.

Withal Harry Truman on the farm displayed a modest interest in politics. Given his part of the country it was of necessity Democratic politics. About the same time, 150 miles to the west in the village of Abilene, Kansas, a youth named Dwight D. Eisenhower was growing up and became a Republican because that was what everyone else was in Eisenhower's part of the country. All the Trumans, except Grandfather Truman who had been a Whig, were

Democrats. When President Grover Cleveland visited Kansas City in 1887, John Truman was a member of the welcoming delegation, riding a big gray saddle horse in front of the reviewing stand, with President Cleveland standing there and everyone cheering. After losing in 1888, Cleveland ran again in 1892 and was reelected to a second nonconsecutive term. During the latter campaign Harry Truman wore a paper hat to school bearing the legend "Cleveland and Stevenson" for the candidate and his running mate. Some big Republican boys took it away from him and tore it up. When victory nonetheless came, Harry's father climbed the cupola of the Independence house and decorated the rooster weathervane. He also rode in the torchlight victory parade.

During the years on the farm Harry Truman was a follower of William Jennings Bryan and went to see him whenever possible. Once he took Bess and was greatly amused, as were the other farmers, when at the meeting out in a field the orator had no platform to stand on, and someone wheeled out a manure spreader. After clambering up on it, Bryan, who was quick-witted, said it was the first time he had ever made a speech from a Republican platform.[8]

In the summer of 1912, Truman was consumed by the race for the Democratic presidential nomination then being contested between Champ Clark, a Missourian and speaker of the House of Representatives, and Governor Woodrow Wilson of New Jersey. His father was for Clark. Harry was for Wilson. On July 2 he was binding wheat in a field of 160 acres, two miles around. Every time he drove around the field he tied the horses and mules—he was driving a four-animal team, two of each—and ran over to the telegraph station along the railroad a quarter of a mile away to see how the convention in Baltimore was going. He was greatly pleased when the convention nominated

Wilson—who was, as it turned out, his Democratic predecessor in drawing up a peace plan after a world war.

Interest in politics was one thing, officeholding something else, and Truman during the farm years hardly had time for that, even though he took a few fliers at minor offices. They are of interest only in retrospect, as training exercises for the politician to come. In 1912, John Truman managed to get on the right side during a furious contest over election of an eastern judge for Jackson County, and after the smoke cleared he became road overseer for the southern half of Washington Township. The son succeeded to the post after the father died. The task was to oversee payment of the poll tax of $3, in lieu of which one could work for three days on the roads or one day if a man brought along a team. There were only a few miles of macadam roads in the township, and all the rest were dirt. Some overseers collected the poll tax money and seldom worked or were easy on individuals who chose to work rather than pay. The Trumans, father and son, were hard on workers. Occasionally the county paid overseers for work on bridges and culverts or for filling mudholes. The Trumans did this custom work with care. But after Harry Truman's appointment, a change in the court cost the son the road job in 1916.

In addition to the few months as road overseer, Truman served for a short time as postmaster of Grandview. He competed for the appointment, which required an examination as well as political support, because a Grandview resident who was after it had agreed to put the office in Dr. Bradford's drugstore, which Truman described as a "booze emporium." Truman took the examination on March 14, 1914, and scored 98 in arithmetic and accounts and a nearly perfect score of 99 in copying addresses; the latter score may have been testimony to the years in the Kansas City banks. His total

J. A. TRUMAN & SON
FARMERS
KANSAS CITY HOME PHONE—HICKMAN 6

GRANDVIEW, MO., _Sept 1_____, 1914

Jackson Co to J. A. Truman Dr
for work on hidge by special order.
J. a. Truman & Teams 2 days working every day
but 4, 13, 18, 19 + 31.   168 00
J. a. Truman & Teams 2 days 4 + 31   32 00
a. W. Rotgell   14 days labor   28 00
Wm Malicoat   24 days labor   48 00
Wm M. Gune   15½ days labor   31 00
Otto Bell   1   "   "   2 00
H. Krueger   2   "   "   4 00
Van Vert   5   "   "   10 00
Ralph Shank   2   "   "   4 00
                                    —————————
                                         3 v 7 °°
Sam Davis 1½   "   "   25 00
                                    $ 352 00

rating was 91.9, which was excellent. Congressman William
P. Borland nominated him and he was appointed in
December 1914, at $503 a year. His term began in
February 1915; he resigned in April, but seems to have
remained until August. However, he did none of the work,
waiving the salary in favor of the assistant, a widow
member of the Hall threshing-machine family who was
helping raise and educate her younger sisters and
brothers. He may have regretted the generosity because
the lost salary (he later wrote) would have paid two farm
hands.[9]

In July 1916, he took the place of U. R. Holmes, who had
resigned, on the board of the Hickman Mills Consolidated
School District No. 1. He served until the following May,

71

but did not run for election for by then he had enlisted in the U.S. Army. The board meetings he attended were hardly earthshattering. The board decided to build a room onto a school if it could do the job for $2,000 or less. It paid teachers' salaries, those of janitors, and miscellaneous bills, one of which was for 75¢. A curiosity of this now forgotten public service is that a contractor for the Holmes Park school building, Murray T. Colgan, with whom the board made a settlement for $166, was Harry Truman's first cousin.

Truman ran for committeeman in Washington Township in the primary of August 1916 and lost.

Books and Music

In addition to all these activities, the farmer near Grandview could escape the loneliness of the farm by widening his intellectual horizons through reading and music. During the evenings, if he didn't have to put his mind to farm matters, problems with crops and the animals, it would have been possible to transport himself from the isolated farm through books and beautiful sounds. He could have purchased books by mail and subscribed to magazines. For musical diversion he had only to turn to the Kimball upright in the parlor or attend concerts in Kansas City.

As a schoolboy in Independence Truman had been a voracious reader and music similarly fascinated him. During his later years in politics he enjoyed a reputation as a well-read man and one who had more than a passing acquaintance with music. But during his years on the farms, he seems to have read few books and his active interest in music languished.

Many years later Truman told Jonathan Daniels that it was not true he spent a great amount of time reading. "My

father," he said, "wouldn't have let me get away with that."[10]
He mainly read light stories in magazines. He admired
Everybody's, which offered short stories and serials, gay
and sad. He and Bess enjoyed a series about a character
known as the Ne'r-Do-Well; the episodes left off at hair-
raising places, leaving readers on needles for the next
issues. He liked the blood and thunder of *Adventure*, none
too adventurous by later standards but full of enough
derring-do to keep tired farmers awake. He read stories by
Mary Roberts Rinehart in *McClure's*. The *Saturday
Evening Post* ran tales about "the infallible Godahl";
versions of Godahl's life appeared in *Pearson's*.

He refused to read articles in farm magazines, which he
considered full of lies. His father tried to get up his
curiosity, and one night, so Harry told Bess, was reading
the farm press aloud for his benefit and for ten minutes
the son did not hear a word. Now and then John Truman
would stop and ask Harry what he thought about "some
exceptionally large lie" he had just read. Harry believed
the owners of the magazines published them for the
advertising money and not for the subscribers. Their
opinions were mostly rot. "They'll tell some long-winded
tale about the great record some guy has made feeding
cattle and at the end you'll find that he's only fed three
and that took all his time and a hired man's. What we want
to know is how to feed a carload and not have anything to
do."[11]

Beyond entertaining short stories he managed a few
popular novels, such as *Keith of the Border*, the sort that
presently fill shelves of secondhand bookstores. These
books contained stories of love, remorse, and death—
happiness and bliss alongside ineffable tragedy, with
tipped-in illustrations of young men in elegant suits and
willowy young ladies in long lacy dresses.

There is little evidence that he read serious books and

enduring works of literature. He did admire Mark Twain, the celebrated writer who died in 1910. That year he bought the Author's National Edition from Harper Brothers in New York, twenty-five books for $25, and paid in monthly installments of $2. The humorist's droll stories, gusto, and admiration for American virtues carried much appeal. Otherwise he seems to have read no books of lasting worth. In the first letter to Bess at the beginning of their courtship, in December 1910, he mentioned a book. "I am very glad you liked the book," he related. "I liked it so well myself I nearly kept it. I saw it advertised in *Life* and remembered that you were fond of Scott when we went to school."[12] It sounds like a book by Sir Walter Scott, but we cannot be sure it was. Bess took pleasure in Dickens and Stevenson and tried to get Harry to read their longer novels. He found them boring, which probably meant they could not keep him awake. His mother admired Alexander Pope, and Harry bought her a copy of Pope's poems for her birthday; but there is no indication he read them. Nor in the correspondence is there evidence that during this considerable period of his life, eleven years, he read anything about history, his principal reading interest when in high school.

Music—the young man's other intellectual interest in Independence in the 1890s—similarly disappeared during the years on the farm. He seldom played the piano. To Bess he mentioned it in passing and made it seem unimportant—he told her that in younger days he had hoped to be an ivory tickler. There were few testimonies to what once had been nearly a passion. The son of a nearby farmer, Gaylon Babcock, remembered how threshers came to the Truman house and after a hard day's work would be sitting around, mostly on the porch, waiting for supper. Harry had duties in its preparation. If he had a little time prior to serving the meal, instead of coming out

A portion of the first letter from Harry Truman to Bess Wallace, 1910.

and "associating with us men" he went in the parlor and played.[13] In a letter to Bess he mentioned playing for the wedding of a cousin in Kansas City. One night at an Eastern Star box social he played for dancing.[14] Otherwise he seems to have given up on the piano. Nor was there much concert-going. While working in the banks he had attended concerts by Ignace Jan Paderewski, Josef Lhevinne, and Vladimir de Pachmann. Harry's teacher, a student of Theodor Leschetizky, once introduced Truman to Paderewski after a concert; Truman said he was having trouble with a turn in the Minuet in G and the pianist sat down backstage at a piano and showed him the turn. But in following years he abandoned pianists in favor of musicals, such as *Floradora*, a hit of the time, and Gilbert and Sullivan operettas, notably *Pinafore*. Harry and Bess also appear to have seen every vaudeville show that came to Kansas City. The letters are full of references to vaudeville.

Courting Bess

It appears, thus, that during the farm years, Harry Truman joined several organizations, but did not read many books or partake of cultural opportunities in Kansas City (although he did go there for musicals and vaudeville). He also extended his life beyond the farm by means of the telephone, railroads, and eventually an automobile—all of which he employed mainly for what beginning in December 1910 became his consuming interest after work hours on the farm: his courtship of Bess Wallace.

The courtship began by chance. He was accustomed to go, now and then, into Independence, ten miles to the east of Kansas City, to visit his cousins, Nellie and Ethel Noland, and their mother, Aunt Ella. It was on one of these visits, after he stayed overnight in the Noland parlor, that he came into the kitchen of the house at 216 North Delaware to discover that Mrs. Wallace, Bess's mother— they lived across the street at 219—had sent over a cake; someone needed to return the plate.

It was a great opportunity. He had met Bess in 1890. He liked to say later that he had fallen in love with her and never really liked another girl. In school they had been in the same classrooms, he had carried her books, and they had studied Latin together at the Noland house. After high school graduation in 1901 they seem to have seen each other no more; the Truman family moved to Kansas City and then to the farm. Bess remained at home to help her mother after her father's suicide in 1903.

Years later the story of the cake plate became a well-worn tale in the Harry Truman family. According to daughter Margaret, her father seized the plate "with something approaching the speed of light" and announced that he would return it. Marching across the street he rang the bell. Luck was with him for Bess answered. She had just divested herself of a boyfriend, and the moment was opportune. "Come in," she said to the Grandview farmer.[15]

Seeking thereafter to advance his cause, he looked for opportunities, which—the Country Life Commission to the contrary—were considerable. Compared to farmers in the past, he was living in a new age. Years later, however, as he recalled that time in his life, he must have smiled wryly over the difficulties, the daunting problems, the troubles that accompanied the mechanical marvels that were offering farmers a life beyond the farm.

Consider the awkwardness of telephoning Bess, which he had to do when farm work forced him to plan visits to Independence at the last moment. Part of the telephone problem was that Kansas City and nearby localities like

Bess—the erstwhile Sunday-schooler, c. 1910.

Bess in 1889, age four.

78

Independence possessed two systems, the Bell and the Home, the latter having arisen out of an antitrust ruling in 1904. The systems did not cooperate and wise merchants advertised: "We're on both phones." Telephoners also had to deal with two books. When Harry was in downtown Kansas City and trying to telephone Bess, he had to find a pay phone on the proper system. For a while, he and Bess were both on the Home system, and then Mrs. Wallace went over to Bell.

After getting the right system it was necessary to go through an operator, and sometimes the operators were smart alecks who sensed they were dealing with a farmer calling his girl. One day Harry said, without thought, "Hello! Bess?" The answer was, "No, this isn't Bess. It's Myrtle."[16] Harry had to contain his exasperation, for to get sharp with "central" could mean more than the usual quota of wrong numbers—obtained after waiting five minutes to get central.

In addition to the problems of a dual phone system and saucy central operators, many friends and neighbors had to share party lines. Truman may have exaggerated when he claimed that ten people were on his country line, but it was often difficult to get through. He said it was necessary to take down the receiver and listen "while some good sister tells some other good sister who is not so wise how to make butter or how to raise chickens or when it is the right time in the moon to plant onion sets or something else equally important." At last the sister would quit "and then if you are quick and have a good, strong voice you can have your say."[17]

After telephoning, the next step was to get there. Trips could turn into nightmares. To go to Independence from Grandview, fifteen miles the way a crow might fly, was much more difficult than to go to Kansas City, twenty miles away. It was necessary to walk a mile to Grandview, which required a half hour, and take the Kansas City Southern to Sheffield, a stop between Kansas City and Independence, then a streetcar to the Independence courthouse square, two blocks from North Delaware Street. Another train line, the Missouri Pacific, came in on the other side of Grandview to the west and thereafter ran parallel to the K. C. Southern. Or one could drive a buggy to Dodson on the southern edge of Kansas City and take an interurban into the city and then a streetcar east the ten miles to Independence. Because one had to leave buggy and horse in a Dodson livery stable and take two cars, that route was far less convenient.

Moreover, the trains of yesteryear, praised by enthusiasts of later times who never rode them, left much to be desired. On January 12, 1912, Truman wrote Bess that the K. C. Southern train left Sheffield on the dot and was two hours late at Grandview. There were twenty passengers, and the car was cold. There was a stove at only one end. A woman and baby were aboard, and the child cried as if it were cold. On August 12 of that same year he went by streetcar from Independence to the downtown Kansas City station at Second and Wyandotte; he avoided Sheffield because several carloads of lumber had upset at Swope Park. The lumber blocked trains from the Wyandotte station, and his train went to a locality named Leeds where he spent the night on a bench. Every minute he thought the train would arrive and that in half an hour he would reach Grandview.[18]

Getting home from Grandview was also a problem. Sometimes luck was with him: A freight got in front of his train as it approached Grandview and slowed it, so he could jump off as it slid past the farm—otherwise he would have had to walk the mile. But whether across fields or out from the village, walking was unsafe, for tramps who rode the rails and got off at small towns and villages to spend the night would sometimes rob farmers. More than once figures whom he presumed to be tramps followed him. He was a slight man and would have made an easy catch.

I had the livin' scared out of me . . . Some guy evidently got off the train as I did. He followed me clear through town a quarter of a mile. Every time I'd whip up he would too, and if I slowed down so did he. I guess he thought I was a bum and I'm sure he was. He finally went south and I went north. I was very much relieved when he did.[19]

There were other scary incidents that he may have exaggerated to impress Bess, but his descriptions were vivid. Once he jumped off the train as it was going around a bend and as he looked across at the farm—the moon was coming up—the barn appeared on fire. After a while he thought it might be a neighbor's house that was on fire; after he got closer, he concluded he was moonstruck.

What Truman needed was an automobile to avoid late trains and moonlight walks. As he wrote Bess, "What I need is a sixty-horse-power motor. Then I could do a day's work and run around all night."[20] In 1914 an opportunity arose to buy a good used automobile and he seized it, purchasing a 1911 model Stafford for $600.

Few Americans today have heard of a Stafford. At one time the United States boasted 2,726 makers of automobiles, and Terry Stafford was one of them. At first he had teamed up with Anton and Clement Smith of Topeka, who owned a firm that produced the Honest John truss, a product designed for hernias. In addition the Smith brothers made artificial limbs, bows and arrows, and Concert Grand Harps. After 1907 they produced the Great Smith Touring Car. That year Stafford resigned as plant superintendent and established his own automobile factory; in 1910 he moved to Kansas City. His cars listed

Two views of the 1911 Stafford. Top: Truman at the wheel, Bess at his side, with Bess's brother Frank holding the pail. In back is Natalie Ott, later Frank's wife, and Mrs. William Southern, the mother of May Wallace. The occasion was a picnic near the Little Blue River, about 1915. Bottom: Harry and Bess in front, Mary Jane and an unidentified friend in back, about 1915. Mary seems to be holding a fishing pole.

new for $2,350. He made 314 of them, and Truman's model was about number 200, a good place in the series. It was a five-passenger open touring car with a top attached by straps to the front part of the frame. It had a windshield mounted in brass and Prestolight lamps. Usually Truman drove it as an open car.

The Stafford made the trips to Independence much easier. It could go sixty miles an hour, if the road allowed. On Sundays, Harry and Bess went for rides of a hundred miles or more. During the first three months Harry drove the car five thousand miles.

Still, trips did not always work out as planned. Automobiles in those days did not run long before the tires blew out, one after another; eight hundred miles were enough for some of those early tires. Other dangers loomed, such as buggies going down the middle of the road at night, the driver asleep, lines tied to the whip, the horse knowing the way but also knowing to walk only in the middle of the road. "I have had to get clear of the road several times," Truman wrote Bess, "to keep from dislocating a wheel."[21] On one occasion he gave in to the importunities of his sister who was learning to drive. Mary managed to careen the car into Grandview, but on return she cut the corner into the lane and knocked the gate off its hinges, bending the car's front axle.

The most bizarre experience with the car fortunately occurred when Bess was not present.[22] One Sunday Harry undertook to drive his mother and Uncle Harrison to Monegaw Springs, eighty miles southeast of Grandview, twenty miles below Clinton. The springs were an attractive place where young and old came, the young to hold hands, the old to think back to when they had come for that purpose. As it turned out, half the fun was getting there, the rest coming back. En route, within half a mile of Monegaw, he ran over a stump and spilled his uncle over the front seat and threw his mother over his own head. No one was hurt, although Uncle Harrison swore like a trooper and may have startled his sister. Harry backed the car off the stump and went on into town with a badly bent axle. He and his mother started home on Monday morning, at 6:00, and after a few miles a rain began. The car began to slip because of the crooked axle and bent steering wheel. Five miles south of Harrisonville it went into the ditch, and the left front wheel was smashed to kindling. They were within a half mile of railroad station by name of Lone Ture; they walked there and Harry telephoned for a wheel. He and his mother sat near the station from 1:30 p.m. until 8:00, waiting for the wheel. When it arrived he could not get it on. The rain commenced again. A farmer came along and took them to his house, where they stayed the night. Next morning the farmer hitched his team to the car and pulled it out of the ditch. By this time Harry had discovered that he had been trying to put the wheel on backward. He went on to Harrisonville and was five miles north of there when he ran through a puddle and got the magneto wet. He telephoned Harrisonville and a man came out, tore it apart, and fixed it. Another farmer meanwhile gave them sustenance—a free meal. Going anywhere in those days, even with the new conveniences, was never an easy task.

CHAPTER IV

The Mortgage

"From the beginning of Indiana to the end of Nebraska there is nothing but corn, cattle, and contentment."

In relating Truman's years on the farm one comes, inevitably, to the subject of the mortgage—that curse of so many farmers in the present century as in earlier farming eras. It is impossible to describe Truman's life on the family farms without discussing the mortgage. And here one looks almost into the center of the family relationships, both his side of the family and that of his wife. One sees again, as in most families, how ambitions, hopes, and heartaches—together with actions—dramatically affected the family fortunes, which in this instance resulted in the inability of the Trumans to keep the Young family farm.

The slow and agonizing business of losing the farm, the watching over a course of years while the farm slipped from the hands of people who had known it in better days, was an experience that seared their lives. In Truman's case the foreclosure that came in 1940 could not have been timed more unfortunately. He was in the midst of the most serious campaign of his entire public career—a political fight if there ever was one. He was in grave danger of losing his Senate seat to an antagonist, Governor Lloyd C. Stark, whom he hated more than any other man he had encountered in his years in politics. As he looked back upon the experience he felt that his political enemies seized upon his troubles over the family farm—along with an acute political problem, to be sure, the collapse of the Pendergast machine in Kansas City—to do him in.

Financial Difficulties

The initial placing of a mortgage on the farm came out of a family argument among the descendants of Grandfather and Grandmother Young, with the Trumans and Uncle Harrison on one side, the other children on

87

the other. At about the same time, Truman began to court Bess Wallace, a seemingly unconnected happening that was nonetheless connected. For in the business of courting Bess the Grandview farmer sought to prove that he was a man of means or imminent means and to convince Bess's mother he was worthy of her daughter. The ventures into which he went to prove himself, ventures apart from his work on the farm, then brought two financial disasters that forced an increase in the farm mortgage.

The argument that led to the mortgage had its origin in the will of Grandmother Young, who died in 1909. When her husband, Solomon, died in 1892 without a will, she had decided to distribute some of his property; she gave each of the seven children 160 acres and divided among them $50,000 or $60,000 in personal property, which allowed several sons-in-law to pay off their debts. Her concern thereafter was that she be able to live out the rest of her days on the farm and not have to go to one of the children's houses or perhaps move to town. The Truman family had already helped out by spending three years on the farm. When they left, Harrison did the farming. In 1895 she drew up a will that gave everything to the two children who had helped; she cut off her other children and their heirs with $5 apiece. Apparently she did not bother to tell the others, and her daughter and son, Martha Ellen and Harrison, did not say anything—if indeed they knew what she had done. After her death, of course, the other children found out. Furious, they brought suit to break the will.

During the trial over Grandmother Young's will, passions rose high. The Trumans underwent the excruciating experience of hearing their close relatives say things in court that were not true; when Aunt Susan Bartleson went on the stand her nephew wrote Bess how he hated to see a "white-haired old lady," whom he liked and

Martha Ellen Truman and Mary Jane, 1916. While living in Commerce, Truman bought the greyhound for Bess. "He is as ugly as a bulldog," he wrote, on August 29. "If he ever grows to his feet, he can outrun a locomotive or Locomobile either" (Dear Bess, p. 211). Evidently Bess's mother or perhaps Bess herself put her foot down, and the dog went to the farm.

respected, "tearing up the truth."[1] It was necessary to show that the Trumans had sought to take the grandmother's money. After the old farmhouse burned, a year after Grandfather Young's death, the grandmother had gone to Independence and lived for a few months with the Trumans until the new house was ready. She arranged her will the next year. The relatives implied that her stay in Independence was part of a plot. They said that after her daughter Martha Ellen moved back to the farm in 1905 she prevented her sisters from visiting their mother. All the while, they said, the grandmother was feebleminded, which may have been true toward the end. A neighbor who was not very friendly to the Truman family, the same Babcock son who had been part of the threshing ring and had listened to Harry play the piano in the parlor, remembered seeing her sitting silently in her room and never heard her say anything on any occasion. But at that time she would have been between the ages of eighty-eight and ninety-one. She made the will when she was seventy-seven, when she should have been in good mind.

After everything nasty was brought out, and the jury deliberated and reported, the result was a nominal victory for the Trumans and Uncle Harrison but a costly cash settlement of $9,500 in favor of the relatives. Moreover, it was necessary for the Trumans to pay a lawyer $3,000. In Harry Truman's correspondence with Bess are passing comments about the lawyer in Kansas City, Fred J. Boxley, a member of the National Guard battery, who took a retainer of $100 a month in addition to court costs and expenses for trips that he made. On one occasion he and Harry went to New Mexico to find a witness to the will and obtain a deposition that Grandmother Young had been in good mind. Before the trip Boxley "politely informed" Harry that $200 were in order. "That guy keeps me busted from month to month," he wrote Bess. "If it keeps up much longer I'm going into the hands of a receiver in Judge Pollock's court." When the case went to trial Boxley's fee rose proportionally, and in a letter of April 2, 1913, Harry related that he was going into Kansas City for a "seance" with the lawyer: "You can perhaps guess what the gentleman wanted. Just a thousand on account."[2]

All this forced Martha Ellen Truman to mortgage the farm for $7,500. She may have received some money from her brother Harrison, who perhaps shared in paying Boxley. He may instead have intimated that he would remember his sister in his will. A crafty fellow, as well as lazy, Harrison very probably did the latter.[3]

Meanwhile the courtship had inspired Harry Truman to prove himself as a farmer with a future, which led to the ventures that eventually affected the mortgage. The proving almost beyond question was not for the sake of Bess but her mother. Mrs. Wallace was the daughter of an Independence man of means, George Porterfield Gates, who years before had joined with a partner to establish a mill that produced Queen of the Pantry Flour, "the best biscuit and cake flour in the world." From this enterprise came a sizable income. In the 1880s, Gates enlarged his house at 219 North Delaware, and behind its pleasant Victorian facade it was possible to count seventeen rooms. At the same time Grandfather Young lived in a colonial-style country mansion and owned two thousand acres and probably could have bought and sold George Gates. But that was beside the point. Mrs. Wallace's experience with her improvident and alcoholic husband persuaded her that her only daughter—Bess had three younger brothers —should marry someone of means. Harry Truman therefore received inspiration to prove himself.

Not long after the beginning of the courtship Truman undertook the first in a series of efforts to display his suitability as a husband for Bess. He took part in a veritable farm raffle, awards by lot of homesteads, sponsored by the federal government to promote settlement of virgin land in South Dakota. Harry went up for the raffle, as required, accompanied by Murray Colgan, the Kansas City cousin whom he later would assist when on the Hickman Mills school board. They took a sleeper to Omaha and there boarded a special train for the north country. Hundreds of farmers went up in long lines of yellow coaches; they sat up all night and sometimes two or three nights. To while away time Harry and Murray played cooncan and seven-up; they took turns getting their meals so they would not lose their seats. At every station they met trains coming back. People shouted to them from the adjoining cars, and the usual gibe was "Sucker!" One farmer advised them to go right through South Dakota to "a very hot place." It was so cold, Harry wrote, that he would not have minded. They arrived at the bleak village of Gregory (not far over the state line), where registration was, at 10:30 in the evening. They had to find a place to stay, which was not easy to do; a hotel man, if one could describe him as such, consented to give them a cot apiece in the "so-called" writing room of the "so-called" hotel, "which was some luxury I tell you."[4] The next day they registered at a wooden shack named the Cow Palace where they encountered twenty notaries inside a hollow square and gave their names and swore to the accuracy of their statements. Harry also registered for a Spanish-American War veteran, so he had a chance to obtain not merely a quarter section (160 acres) but half of another if the veteran won. The government had arranged the lottery so that there were prizes of different value, ranging from land worth between $8,000 and $12,000 down to several thousand parcels of value ranging from $40 to $4,000.

When neither Harry's name nor his veteran friend's came up for South Dakota, he tried another lottery at

Glasgow, Montana. In 1913 the federal government opened 1.3 million acres of the Fort Peck Indian Reservation in the northeastern part of the state, and twelve thousand people registered for 8,405 homesteads of 160 acres. Truman, his father, brother, the threshing-machine operator, Leslie Hall, two of Hall's sons, Gaylon Babcock, and Grandview veterinarian Ed Young went. Over the winter of 1913–1914, several individuals around Grandview who were interested in the land held meetings, which Truman described to Bess as the Fort Peck Settlers Association. He wrote that he might become governor of Montana and asked if she would like to be Mrs. Governor.[5] Word came that he was in luck, having drawn claim 6,199. Real estate men began to write, offering location services for $50, even though the reservation was fifty miles by a hundred, six times larger than Jackson County. He began to be skeptical and thought he would have as much luck, without spending $50, if he shut his eyes and put his finger on the map of Montana. Then he heard about the climate. In early May 1914, it snowed seven inches in South Dakota, and he reasoned that no such snow would have the "impudence" to "miss the great state of Montana." Over the winter the temperature there, he learned, had gone down to 47° below. The wind, someone said, blew sixty miles an hour right out of Alaska. "I guess I can get me a cowskin cloak and a beaver cap and manage to keep warm." Coal was $2 a ton in Montana, but each resident, he guessed, burned seventy tons a week.[6] He decided not to accept his claim.

During these attempts to impress Bess's mother and win her daughter, Harry Truman sought to persuade Uncle Harrison to "let loose" of some money so that the two, nephew and uncle, might make a speculation. They looked over the proposal of a Kansas City inventor of an ice machine. The idea was attractive; this was still the time when people quarried ice off ponds, packed it in sawdust, and stored it in barns. But Harrison backed away—sensing that none of them—he, Harry, or the inventor—knew anything about ice machines. The two also went to Texas to look over land, and Harry was impressed, and so at first was his uncle; but after several days on the train, listening to land salesmen and hearing from owners who had bought land two or three years earlier who said Texas was an American Eden, Harrison began to make jokes about Texas. He told Harry that if the nephew would stick to Texas when it was dry, Texas would stick to him when it was wet. The uncle soon gave up on Texas land.

For a while Truman was almost persuaded to try Texas land on his own. A Texan, Oscar K. Herndon, offered him 160 acres on his word for five years or a section on the same terms. The land was in West Texas. To a perhaps skeptical Bess he wrote from Fort Worth, "I suppose you think that I am somewhat erratic in my Texas trips. I am, but there is method in my madness." He told her what she knew, that he was impatient at "my slow progress at home." Prospects had been bright until "one disaster after another has almost put me in the bad." The Texas proposition had "a fine face on it." Herndon said Truman could get someone to run the Texas farm and could make a large stake in a short time. It was tempting, Harry wrote, because as things stood he did not even have enough money to buy Bess a ring.[7]

Like the first Texas hope, the second did not turn out. It was a gamble, and the Missouri farmer was not up to it. Actually he was better off not taking it, despite the fact that land prices went up after the United States entered World War I. Prices of commodities farmers needed to buy went up even more, and land prices tumbled after the war.

In 1916 Truman invested in a lead and zinc mine in Commerce, Oklahoma, near the Missouri border; it failed.

For months he tried to keep the mine going, an intensely difficult task involving the supervision of several miners and a mine boss. The mine workers gave trouble of one sort or another and he fired one group only to try another without any better luck. It was necessary to keep the mine pumped out, and the pump's boiler often failed. "Things are somewhat mixed here," he wrote Bess, "and I'm the official straightener."[8] His partners were no help. One was a scamp named Jerry Culbertson who never would do any work and spent his time in Kansas City. Another was a neighboring farmer named Thomas R. Hughes, but when lightning struck his barn he abandoned interest in the T.C.H. Mining Company. Harry Truman had to commute to Commerce from Grandview, from the top of Missouri's western border to the bottom, 192 miles, "and about 92 of them are as rough as a road can be." There were four river bottoms full of chuckholes, for the Stafford to cross.[9] The train trip was not much easier. He tried to keep the farm going with hired help. The farm was in Mary's charge, and the hands did not like working for a woman. Harry wired saying the men should cut the clover, Mary passed the instruction, and the men told her they were going to finish plowing for corn. Mary fired them, they laughed and said, "When Harry gets home he'll take us back." And Harry rushed home from Commerce and hired two new hands in Kansas City.[10] In the end it became obvious the mine was a failure. Truman took his lumps—$7,500 worth, which he borrowed from his mother.[11]

Just before this dark moment, Uncle Harrison died. The uncle willed $500 each to two of the sisters and his brother and $250 each to a nephew (Solomon Chiles) and two nieces (Elizabeth Waskom and Suda Wells). He gave his half of the farm, three hundred acres, to Martha Ellen Truman and her three children. Uncle Harrison's bequest

Harry Truman, oilman, in 1916, perhaps standing over the Teter Pool.

meant that Harry Truman now owned a fourth of the uncle's part of the family farm, seventy-five acres; but this hardly made him a wealthy man.

In a last and, as it turned out, futile effort to obtain money, Truman became secretary of a wildcat oil company, known variously as Morgan and Company and Atlas-Okla Oil Lands Syndicate. The company put down a 900-foot well in Greenwood County, Kansas. Had the partners drilled deeper they could have tapped into the famous Teter Pool and become millionaires. They ran out of money, closed operations, and the Cities Service Oil Company tapped the pool.[12]

Exactly how much the oil venture cost Truman is difficult to say, for its financing has never become clear. Most of the investors were individuals to whom the company's officers—the wildcatter David H. Morgan, Truman, and the untrustworthy Jerry Culbertson—sold stock certificates. The investors, of course, lost everything. Even today, decades after the operation closed down, there are people in Kansas who say Harry Truman bilked their relatives out of hard-earned money for worthless stock. Of the organizers, Morgan contributed his expertise, which was considerable; he was a competent oilman, who remained in the business for the rest of his life. Culbertson was primarily the salesman who would sell anything to anyone. Truman issued stock certificates and kept the office going in Kansas City. For his financial share in starting the company he contributed $5,000 in notes cosigned by his mother. He may have contributed more. In a settlement after the war he took title to a house in Kansas City, which he exchanged for a farm in nearby Johnson County, Kansas. The farm had a mortgage but his interest was considerably beyond that at current prices. He put up the farm as collateral for a note signed during the life of the ill-fated haberdashery, and the bank that held the note took the farm as part payment on the note. The amount that the bank took off the note, if anything, is unknown (Truman averred that the Johnson County farm paid the note, although in 1935 he bought the note at auction for $1,000; by that time the nominal value of the note was $8,900). Meanwhile, over the winter of 1916–1917, he seems to have received a salary for his office work, and it might have offset some of the money he contributed.

By now Martha Ellen Truman found herself crowded financially, having supported Harry in his lead and zinc venture and in the oil venture. In February 1917, she increased the home farm mortgage to $25,000.

The Foreclosure

Thus, by 1917 the farm was heavily mortgaged. Truman then added to the problems by entering the army and, after the war, marrying Bess and moving his residence to Independence. His departure took away the farm's stability—its management.

That Truman would go into the army, once the United States declared war, could have been predicted. His intense patriotism made staying out impossible. He was in no danger of being drafted; he was thirty-three and a farmer. He signed up with his old battery in Kansas City and undertook to help enlarge the unit into a regiment. He worked so hard to persuade men to enlist, he later said, that he told his comrades they ought to make him a sergeant. They made him a first lieutenant.[13] After induction into federal service the regiment went by train to Fort Sill, Oklahoma, to a cantonment on the Sill reservation known as Camp Doniphan. In April 1918, Harry Truman took the trip "across the pond" and during the war's last months saw hard service on the front.

One might also have predicted that the war would widen his horizons. Once again, as during the six years in the National Guard, he enjoyed associating with men his own age, despite his annoyance with regular army officers and the army's extraordinary ways of accomplishing ordinary tasks. He enjoyed the chance for leadership that came to him as an officer. Promoted to captain, he received command of Battery D, a unit of 196 men. First in a quiet sector in the Vosges, then as Saint-Mihiel and the Meuse-Argonne, he showed he could handle men; he was very effective as a battery commander.

The war gave him an excuse (which he hardly needed, as he had been discovering them for years) to urge Bess to marry him. This time Mrs. Wallace could not ask him to demonstrate that he could support Bess. With Mrs.

98

Wallace's blessing the two agreed that they would tie the knot as soon as the war was over.

Marriage ensured that Truman would not go back to the farm. Bess would not have allowed it: She heartily disliked the farm. When they were courting she had gone out once in a while, but her visits were infrequent. Harry knew she liked tennis and laboriously constructed a dirt court next to the farmhouse; but even though he told her all about the labor involved he could not get her to come out and play. A town girl, she saw nothing interesting in the farm.

And so after a wedding trip to Chicago, Detroit, and Port Huron, Bess took Harry back to 219 North Delaware, where with exception of hotel rooms, rented apartments in Washington, and the White House, he maintained his residence for the rest of his life.

Meanwhile he decided to open a men's furnishing store, a haberdashery. While in France he had talked with a member of his regiment, Sergeant Edward Jacobson, about opening a store in downtown Kansas City. Jacobson had helped him run a successful canteen at Camp Doniphan. To raise money to sock the haberdashery Truman held a sale of his farm implements and farm animals. He also sold his one-eighth share of the farm to his mother. A story in the *Independence Examiner* described the events.

Capt. Harry Truman has decided to quit farming for the present. With his mother and sister he owns a 600-acre farm a mile north of Grandview and they have leased the land in several tracts. They are holding an all-day auction of the farm property, hogs, horses, cattle and farming implements. Capt. Truman is going into business in Kansas City.[14]

Even with the move to town (which was common among farmers all over the country after World War I) and the opening of the haberdashery in November 1919, it might still have been possible to watch over the farm, fifteen miles away, by giving advice to hired men or supervising renters. The mortgage could have been slowly reduced from the height it had reached in 1917. In retrospect, because Truman so deeply resented the foreclosure twenty years later and because the farm meant so much to him in memories and in lessons learned, he should have done this, even though he no longer possessed any of the acreage.

But another factor intervened: the heady feeling that farmers and former farmers possessed at this time, a feeling that all was well, that everything was right with farming. In the years when Truman was on the farm, and for some time thereafter, farmers were full of their future. Despite the usual farm catastrophes (and Truman and other farmers all knew about them), everything on American farms seemed to be getting better and better. Shortly after the turn of the century an Iowa orator said, "From the beginning of Indiana to the end of Nebraska there is nothing but corn, cattle, and contentment." In his annual report of 1909, Secretary of Agriculture James Wilson wrote, "The value of the farm products is so incomprehensively large that it has become merely a row of figures." The Country Life Commission declared, despite its lugubrious estimates, "There has never been a time when the American farmer was as well off as he is to-day, when we consider not only his earning power, but the comforts and advantages he may secure." Sometimes the estimates turned to spread-eagleism. According to one observer, "One American harvest would buy the kingdom of Belgium, king and all; two would buy Italy; three would buy Austria-Hungary; and five, at a spot-cash price, would take Russia from the czar."[15]

Figures for Truman's farm years bore out these

100

estimates. His years on the farm had been farming's veritable golden age. If 1899 is regarded as 100 for prices of farm produce, 1910 brought prices of 189.2. After 1910 the steady rise was arrested, but receipts were excellent compared to the 1890s. In 1914 wheat brought 80¢ a bushel, corn 60¢ to 70¢; in the 1890s wheat sold for from 50¢ to 60¢, corn 25¢ to 30¢.[16]

The value of improved farm land rose rapidly. From 1900 to 1910 it increased by 118.1 percent. In Missouri the rise was not quite so good, but good enough: 107.9. Like farmers everywhere, Truman believed the value of land would continue to rise. Grandfather Young had made money by buying at the government price of almost nothing and waiting for prices to go up; much of the money he possessed at the time of his death had come from rising land values. A Truman neighbor bought acreage from Aunt Laura Everhart in 1902 that Solomon Young entered in 1852 or thereabouts at $1.25 per acre; the neighbor paid $40. Jackson County land was rising faster than other Missouri land because of proximity to Kansas City. It was the highest-priced agricultural land in the state. Average prices per acre rose from $71 in 1900 to $125 in 1910. In 1914, Truman believed the farm could bring $200 an acre.[17]

If the latter evaluation, $200 an acre, was accurate, who could see danger in a mortgage of $25,000 on six hundred acres of prime Jackson County land? The family farm was worth $120,000! In the same letter in which he ventured that the farm was worth $200 an acre, he predicted that in four or five years it might bring $600. That meant $360,000!

After listening to the paeans about farm income and the value of acreage and observing the reality between 1900 and 1914—farm land continued to go up through 1914—farmers thought everything would go on rising.

Between 1900 and 1910 the real price of farm land jumped 6 percent a year, the greatest rise in United States history except perhaps during the 1790s and the 1970s.[18]

But then the price cycle for acreage turned down—and with a vengeance. For years thereafter, it moved ever downward until 1942. Slowly at first, not always in nominal dollar value, the worth of land declined steadily. In the 1920s farm income appeared all right. Inflation during and after World War I gave the impression of big gains in value of acreage. But in 1960 dollars of consumer purchasing power the figures for the value of improved farm land in the United States as a whole showed a marked decrease from a nominal value of $33.14 in 1910 to $22.59 in 1940. In 1960 New England consumer dollars, this was a drop from $103.08 to $47.72. For the west north-central states, including Missouri, which has better farm land than the national average, the figures were even worse. In 1910, in 1960 New England consumer dollars, the average value was $136.22; by 1940 it was $57.64.

In the United States as a whole, the overall peak-to-trough, 1914–1942, was 59 percent, 3.16 percent a year. Land values did not match the golden year of 1914 until 1965. In the west north-central states, land values did not match 1914 until the 1970s.[19]

No wonder that when farmers looked back they called the period when Truman was a farmer the golden age and that when the agriculturist George N. Peek in the early 1920s began to agitate for what he and his collaborator, Brigadier General Hugh S. Johnson, described as "parity," they meant the period between 1909 and 1914.[20]

No wonder that, in the 1920s and 1930s, Truman tended to dream of his farm years and, having left the farm, failed to sense the realities of farm economics, the impossibility of return to the golden age, save by intervention of the government in Washington, as happened with the first

New Deal Agricultural Act in 1933. But then the New Deal measures and those of subsequent administrations moved away from parity toward a confusion of purposes, giving the farmers just enough to keep them politically quiet, until enough farmers had left the farm that even such recourses no longer were necessary.[21]

During the bad years of the 1920s and 1930s the Truman farm mortgage could have been a crude barometer of the farm's health; if Harry Truman did not understand the more than halving of the acreage's real value between 1914 and 1942 he might have watched the size of the mortgage. It should have gone down. Instead the family paid only the interest until 1938, when they consolidated a $3,000 lien from 1933 and a $5,500 second mortgage given by the Kansas City Life Insurance Company into a new mortgage of $35,000.

Moreover, in preceding years the family sold off more than half the land. They sold house lots and leased a lot for a gasoline station—Grandview was moving out toward the farm. This reduced the farm to 287 acres.

The Trumans—which, in terms of the farm, meant two households, Vivian, his wife, and five children, and Mamma Truman and Mary—were clearly using the farm as a sort of bank. The family received crop income from the farm (the usual arrangement with renters was to divide income after seed and other expenses, although they may have received cash rent). It did not suffice, so they sold parcels. It is difficult to know how much came in from them. In the president's later papers is a summary of an abstract for the farm, drawn in 1950, that shows sales but no considerations.[22] The lots presumably did not bring in enough, so the family arranged the lien and second mortgage. When they consolidated the farm's debts into the new mortgage, they added $1,500, perhaps for unpaid interest on the smaller loans or for cash for living expenses.

During this period Truman himself was in no position to help with the farm's finances. Part of the reason was a succession of debts, the most serious of which was caused by the closing of the haberdashery in 1922 with a loss of $30,000. Eddie Jacobson could not pay any of the partnership's debts and went bankrupt in 1925; Truman avoided bankruptcy only because he was a county official and creditors could not enforce judgments against him. He managed to pay off the haberdashery debt in 1935 by buying back a note at a sheriff's sale for $1,000 that originally was worth $5,600 and had increased to $8,944.78 because of unpaid interest; the bank that held it in 1935 was a successor to a failed bank and had gotten it at a discount, perhaps almost nothing, and was willing to sell it cheaply. But the year before he had gone back into debt, borrowing from a life insurance policy to campaign for the Senate. Repaying the new loan over the next years, he again went into debt in 1940 for the campaign for reelection.

But this was only part of the reason why he struggled, year after year, to get ahead of debts and in essence failed, albeit short of bankruptcy. During the 1920s and 1930s his income from the county court and then the Senate was considerable for the time. His relatives, however, and Bess's, were not doing well, and he seems to have helped some of them—certainly his mother and sister and probably others. The records in the library in Independence do not say much about his, and one can only add up his income during those years and note mostly modest expenditures (Bess was a bit of a spender who sometimes ran up department store charges) and wonder how many relatives he was helping. Whatever income he had left, after juggling his debts, must have gone to the relatives. After those disbursements there was nothing left to help save the farm.

The Mortgage

In 1938 a wealthy director of the Bank of Belton, Anna Lee Rosier, who in 1932 had bought the farm mortgage from the bank, doubtless to enable the bank to stay open during the depression, asked the Trumans to find another holder, which Vivian did by going to the county school board. The latter possessed legal authority to invest surplus funds in real estate loans. Two Pendergast judges were on the county court, and they arranged to take the mortgage when their anti-Pendergast colleague, unfriendly to the arrangement, was out of the courtroom.

The school board loan went through in April 1938, and from the outset it was an implausible, really impossible proposition. For one thing it had the odor of a political fix; the board had never bought a mortgage before and did not do so again. For another, it probably was illegal because the Trumans did not fulfill one of the parts of the contract. It was necessary to have signatures from two residents of Jackson County who testified that the loan was a reasonable investment, and in case it went into default they were bound to reimburse the county for any loss. The Trumans, including the senator, appear to have taken this requirement lightly. Vivian was one of the signers, and his net worth must have been slight or negative. The other signer was an assistant to the senator, Fred Canfil, who like the senator's brother probably could not have guaranteed anything. Vivian later said that he had bought a bond; who gave a bond for such a purpose is unrecorded. Moreover, the loan was supposed to be repaid by the end of the year with 6 percent interest. An unofficial appraisal of the farm that year, with its reduced acreage, gave its value as $22,680. The farm's buildings—by this time a decrepit house and equally decrepit barn and outbuildings—could not have made up the difference between appraisal and mortgage; indeed in the Middle West farms are always appraised with their buildings.

105

By December 31, 1938, the Trumans were in default for principal, interest, and taxes.

The negotiations went on for a year and a half, during which time the Trumans paid nothing. The senator sought in vain to find a buyer. At last, in the summer of 1940, when the county court had changed complexion and included another anti-Pendergast judge, it foreclosed.

For Senator Truman June 1940 was the worst possible time, for he was in a tight primary race with Governor Stark. One of the senator's lieutenants cannily enticed District Attorney Maurice Milligan, the man who had prosecuted Boss Tom Pendergast, into the race, to split the "good government" votes; but Truman could not be sure of success. Pendergast had been caught red-handed and sent to Leavenworth for having taken a massive bribe from several dozen national fire insurance companies in order to get them a favorable ruling from the state insurance director who was in his pocket. Scores of Pendergast's henchmen similarly went to jail. Because of his close ties with the boss, the senator was clearly vulnerable, and Stark—and Milligan—wanted his seat.

Everything seemed to be collapsing. The senator's campaign chest was empty. President Roosevelt stopped just short of endorsing Stark, and through an intermediary, Press Secretary Stephen T. Early, offered the senator a high-salaried appointment to the Interstate Commerce Commission. Truman indignantly refused, telling an associate who was on the telephone with Early to tell the secretary to tell the president to go to hell.

In the summer of 1940, Truman fought for his political life and won the primary by an 8,400-vote plurality that involved some fast footwork in St. Louis. He won despite bad publicity about the farm mortgage, which his enemies claimed he had foisted off on the school board. He chose to believe that they had sought to do him in by smearing him. For the rest of his life he hated the two anti-Pendergast county judges. He also blamed the real estate developer in Kansas City, J. C. Nichols, whom he had dealt with, not always gently, when he himself was presiding judge of the county court. One of Nichols's subordinates had put the low appraisal on the farm in 1938. Insult was added to injury when Mamma Truman and Mary moved off the farm—as the senator put it: His mother and sister were "run off." The two women moved into an unfamiliar house in Grandview, and Truman's eighty-seven-year-old mother fell down the stairs and broke her hip. She recovered, but two more falls in the next years caused hip fractures that brought her death in 1947.

The Land Is Sold

The Truman farm came up at sheriff's sale early in 1945, when its erstwhile farmer was vice president. Three Kansas City friends—E. Kemper Carter, Charles F. Curry, and Tom L. Evans—bought it, and the Trumans bought it from them. At last the home place was back in familiar hands. By then Harry Truman was no longer in debt, having become solvent during the war years and having paid off his last loan for the senatorial race of 1940. The Democratic National Committee took care of the vice presidential race in 1944. But the new vice president had none too large a bank account, and when his friends purchased the farm for $43,500, Truman was only able to handle part of the deal. They sold him eighty-seven acres for $20,000 and kept the remaining two hundred.[23] Next year, as president, with more income, he bought the rest.

Front view of the Truman home near Grandview, Mo.

After Mamma Truman and Mary Jane left the farm in 1940 the farmhouse fell into disrepair. Courtesy Kansas City Star.

Truman calculated that the county's ownership of the farm did not cost taxpayers a cent, and in later years often made the point. Sale of the property was at $43,500. Income had been $4,865.94. Total receipts hence were $48,365.94. The amount of the loan was $35,000. Gross gain was $13,365.94. After the county deducted maintenance cost of $2,444.96, net gain was $10,920.98.[24]

In actual fact the county lost much more than the onetime farmer estimated it gained. He failed to calculate inflation; a 1938 dollar was worth $1.27 in 1945; for the 1938 mortgage of $35,000 the county needed $44,450. He did not add interest at 6 percent, which when compounded equaled $17,635. He did not add foreclosing costs, a minimum of $200. The county thus required $62,285. Net crop income was $2,420.98 (in 1940–1945 dollars of indeterminate value). Sale price was $43,500. Loss to the county was $16,364.02.[25]

Thereafter two of Vivian's sons, Harry and Gilbert, farmed the acreage until the family sold it off. In 1958, Truman, his brother, and sister, with whom he shared ownership, sold 220 acres in what the *Kansas City Star* called the "Big Truman Land Deal" to a developer, B. F. Weinberg, for a shopping center and other commercial developments, together with multiple-unit housing and from five hundred to six hundred single-family houses to be known as Truman Village. The developer planned houses in the $14,500 to $25,000 range; all were to have full basements and most were to be air-conditioned. The Trumans sold the 220 acres for $1,000 an acre.[26]

Reduction of the acreage to a shadow of what it once was, not to mention all the development, bothered Harry Truman, but there was nothing he could do about it. "I had expected to rebuild the old farm home out at Grandview," he explained in an interview, "as it was when my grandfather and grandmother—both of my grandfathers lived there—and my mother and father lived there, but conditions developed and the development of these places in the country, where people shop, these shopping centers, so it couldn't be done." He said that every time he went by there, he had "a very nostalgic feeling . . . I used to sow wheat . . . and harvest wheat and help my father and brother to thresh it and plant corn and gather it in the same place where this shopping center is now." It was no longer, he confessed, "the old home which was established by my grandfather." It was part of the city. That happened, he said, and one had to accept it.[27]

At this juncture the two barns of the old farmstead—there was the big barn and a smaller hay barn—seemed almost superfluous. The other outbuildings had disappeared; perhaps Vivian's sons had knocked them down or they rotted and collapsed. The hay barn was the first to go. The construction company for Truman Corners Town and Country Shopping Center used it for offices and storage and then dismantled it. The larger barn had been used by Vivian's sons for storage. Vivian knew about the walnut wood and was fond of presenting mementos to friends in the form of gavels and canes carved by an Independence friend. The friend made a high chair for one of Margaret Truman Daniel's sons. One morning in 1966 a trucker arrived at the barn to unload eight horses he had brought from Arkansas and noticed in its recesses a faint glow, a soft red spot. When he opened the door he saw more than a glow—it was a fire about to turn into a conflagration. Some boys apparently had been playing or smoking in the barn and had set straw on fire. He called the Grandview fire department, but by the time the firemen arrived they could do nothing. The fire had taken hold and was belching black clouds of smoke, and the huge timbers of walnut and elm turned into oblongs of red-hot fire, then to embers, with the cedar shingles going up last, looking like flaming plates sailing into the fields. The workplace of Trumans and Youngs passed into history.[28]

In subsequent years the Trumans sold off small pieces of the acreage held back from the developer, until twenty acres were left, containing the farmhouse. The latter deteriorated, even though a couple lived in it. The paint peeled; the front porch rotted and sagged; siding curled as unpainted boards drew water and opened. The roof leaked. Everything around the house looked desolate. The last of the maples went down in the tornado of 1957 and volunteer trees remained, together with underbrush the Trumans sometimes mowed.

Eventually a large restaurant company offered to buy the house, build a restaurant on the back, and use the shell of the house for a cocktail lounge. This proposal shocked the Truman family, the townspeople in Grandview, and citizens of Jackson County; at that point events took a turn for the better. A group of Grandview townspeople and county citizens began to raise money to save what they described as the Truman farm home. In 1980, the United States Department of the Interior awarded the group $378,250 for purchase of 5.3 acres including the farmhouse. This sale was arranged with the Trumans; the appraised value of the land was much higher. To renovate the farmhouse, which was designated a national historic landmark in 1985, the Jackson County legislature, successor to the county court, appropriated $81,000; the Missouri Department of Natural Resources gave $25,000; and the Grandview Board of Aldermen donated $5,000. A retired carpenter volunteered to put the house in shape. An archaeologist traced the foundations of nearby out-buildings, perhaps in hope that someday they could be reconstructed. On June 28, 1987, the county opened the house to visitors.[29]

By this time the farmhouse was surrounded, virtually engulfed, by fast-food restaurants and gasoline stations. Nearby was a large nursing home. As one drove along the street, awash with cars and pickup trucks, it was possible to miss the Truman farm home. It could be found if one looked carefully, however, and turned up a little driveway and circled around.

The present was a far cry from the past. But at least a portion of the onetime family farm, the house, was preserved. And well it should have been, considering the people who once lived there.

*As far as the eye could see there were the fields.   Photograph by
Bradley Smith.*

CHAPTER V

Once a Farmer

"It was on the farm that Harry got his common sense. He didn't get it in town."

There are two important questions concerning Harry Truman's years on the farm. One is What sort of farmer was he? The inquiry is necessary, for when Truman became president there was much talk of how good a farmer he was—talk generated by both his political supporters and by the idolaters who surround every president of the United States. One even suspects among the celebrants the many Americans who saw a true farm figure—a man who had been close to agriculture—and who knew that not many presidents had any acquaintance with farm life and that the numbers of farmers were rapidly decreasing. These farm enthusiasts, one might call them, swept down on Truman the former farmer and seized him, held him up, paraded his connection with the American farm, commented enthusiastically on every remark or trace of experience that related to rural ways. As soon as he became president, reporters scurried to friends and neighbors in Missouri and asked what they remembered. They all said he was an excellent farmer. Years later, after Truman had died, Niel Johnson of the library staff in Independence interviewed Grandview and farm people who had known Truman, even vaguely; every one of the reminiscences was laudatory. One man recalled Truman standing on a farm wagon and pitching bundles into the hopper of the threshing machine. The future president was helping a youngster who had tired from the exhausting work. And when Truman threw the bundles into the machine he pitched them headfirst, which ensured that no grain would be lost.[1]

In answering the question about farming ability it is perhaps best to divide the issue. To decide how technically competent he was is not so difficult a task. He appears to have possessed a considerable aptitude for farming. He combined a knack, or bent, for the work with the necessary enthusiasm and enjoyment and ability to work—to be effective any knack or bent has to have the latter accompaniments. All this was evident in the letters to Bess, in which he reported plowing, sowing, planting, cultivating, reaping. He was doing what he liked or he would not have written about it in such detail; if he had been writing to keep in touch his letters could have been much shorter. Moreover, as a farmer he displayed inventiveness. Contemporaries knew him as a "figurin'" farmer, always thinking about how to do things. Some of this came to him through his father, but a good deal of it was his own—not merely picking up the manure from the Grandview barns and stables and spreading it on the clover fields, which he did with his father, but running the cultivator shortly after sowing wheat or oats to get a head start on the weeds.

As for more general farming ability, what one might describe as good judgment, his record stood revealed in the farm's annual income, the bottom line, which was impressive. Harry told Bess that the home place netted $6,000 or $7,000 each year. He told Jonathan Daniels (and his daughter repeated the figure in one of her books) that the farm netted $15,000, although he may have been thinking of gross income or may have doubled the net to allow for inflation from 1906 through 1917 until he talked to Daniels in 1949.[2] The former figures sufficed to make the farm stand out as a producer. The latter amounted to a substantial income if it represented dollars of that time.

In regard to the farm there remains the fact that neither he nor his parents could ever save any money and went deeply into debt during the years after his father's death. Stephen Slaughter, son of one of the neighbors, wrote that the Trumans could not keep what they made. "You know," he said, "they didn't have much spare money. The Trumans were always strapped."[3] This fact raises a question beyond technical ability at farming or ability to produce income.

It is necessary at this point to discount the testimony of Gaylon Babcock who, when he gave library archivists an oral history, blamed Truman for the increases in the mortgage beginning in 1917 and the farm's eventual foreclosure.[4] For one thing, Babcock was not a neutral witness. He was irritated because of a run-in his father had years before with Harry Truman. When the latter was on the farm the elder Babcock had lent money to a Grandview bartender, and John Truman cosigned the note. The bartender absconded. For some reason Babcock senior did nothing about the note for ten years and then asked payment from the presiding judge of Jackson County, who in a dictated letter not merely refused—as he should have, for it was not his note—but was curt about it and close to rude.

The younger Babcock also said he knew Vivian Truman well and that Vivian had talked to him many times about how Harry had been shrewd with his mother, borrowing money for ventures. This is a more interesting commentary. Vivian may, in fact, have made such a remark. The younger Truman brother was quite a different man from the Truman who rose to be eastern judge, presiding judge, senator, vice president, president. When the two worked together in the Kansas City banks, Vivian showed no aptitude for the work and his brother did well, even though Harry was hardly dedicated to it. Whatever Vivian tried did not turn out too well. Over the years discouragement may have set in, and when talking with an old neighbor he might have made "cracks" about his far better known brother.

But if Vivian did say what Gaylon Babcock credited him with, he failed to understand the situation on the farm. Vivian had left in 1911 to take up his own farm, and

Harry and their father stayed on. Harry helped keep the place going, and after John Truman died he was the sole manager. It was the same situation when Grandmother Young received help first from Uncle Harrison and then the Trumans. In 1914, Martha Ellen put up the $600 to buy the Stafford; whether Harry paid her back is unclear—he may not have. She supported him in his venture in lead and zinc and then in oil. During the former she told him that his grandfather, her father, had "gone broke" three times she knew of and always came back.[5] She supported him doggedly, and Truman wrote Bess about it, saying he had two supporters: his mother and her. If only because he had helped his mother, she was willing to go down the line for him.

More to the point has been the criticism of the younger Slaughter, who has said in a book about his family and in an oral history that the Trumans made several special errors of judgment on the farm that kept them from getting ahead and that ensured their eventual loss of the home place.Stephen Slaughter's commentaries offer an explanation for the Trumans' failure on the farm, despite ability. He admitted that John Truman and his son were excellent farmers. But he said they were not as imaginative as they should have been. They did not put a windmill on their barn cistern, nor did they erect a silo to feed cattle in winter. They had too many hired men. Their outlook never stretched beyond farming—they could not seize opportunities. About the time Harry Truman went to the farm, O. V. Slaughter helped organize the Farmers Bank of Grandview, later went into dairying, and when it became clear that Kansas City could expand only to the south, the Slaughters held their land.[6]

Unlike Gaylon Babcock, Stephen Slaughter had no score to settle. He liked the Trumans. His father had helped them win the court case against the relatives by testifying in their favor. Afterward one of the jurors told O. V. Slaughter that if he had not gone on the stand, the jury would have voted against the Trumans. The next year on a sad Sunday afternoon when John Truman was dying, the Slaughters had gone over to see him and his wife, and the older Truman confessed to them that he had been a lifelong failure. O. V. spoke up strongly to his friend and told him he had not been a failure.[7]

And yet Stephen's points about the Trumans' errors in farming are not as convincing as they might appear. Offered without malice, in long retrospect, by a scion of a farm family who like his brothers left the Slaughter family farm for a successful career elsewhere (as a commercial photographer in New York City), his judgment of the Trumans nonetheless appears mistaken. The comments about the windmill and silo make little sense if one looks at them closely; absence of these items on the Truman farm probably meant little or nothing. In the first decade of the present century a farmer could buy a windmill from the Sears, Roebuck catalog for $15. Catalog pages, reprinted for modern readers, are replete with pictures of windmills that today can be seen as derelicts on farms across the country, victims to electric motors bought during the 1930s and 1940s. The pictures excite later readers and could have excited Stephen when he saw the reality on his own farm. Perhaps the Truman barn cistern did not hold enough water to make even the small investment worthwhile. As for the silo, maybe the Trumans sold their cattle before winter or did not have enough to make a silo pay. In addition, Harry detested loading a silo, thought it unbearable to tramp around in a circle where the dust was thick, and it is possible he refused to build one for that reason.[8] As for the hired-man contention, it was unfair to the Trumans who could get no work out of Uncle Harrison, could not prevent Vivian from leaving, and of course could do nothing to prevent the death of John Truman in 1914. Stephen remarked that his family had only one hired man, which was true, but neglected to say that his father had four sons who stayed on the farm until they went to college. The latter point brings to mind the remark of John D. Hicks about family farms—that the larger the farm's crop of boys and girls, the better.[9]

The comments he made about banking, dairying, and holding the land similarly did not prove that Harry Truman lacked farsighted farm judgment. Unlike O. V. Slaughter, Harry could not have gone into banking during his first years on the farm for Grandmother Young owned the land; he and his family had come to the farm almost penniless. Harry left the farm before the Slaughters were able to turn to dairying. In regard to holding the land, the Slaughters were correct to do it; the Trumans the opposite, but again by that time Harry was off the farm. Stephen has also not stressed a windfall for the Slaughters, in which the Trumans had no opportunity to share. The railroad took a right of way through the Slaughter farm, separating the barn from the house, and the Slaughters took the railroad for $50,000, a princely sum in those days and even now.[10]

Nevertheless, when Stephen Slaughter reminisced about the Trumans, speculated about why they did not get ahead financially over the long run, and touched the issue of their farming ability, he raised one point that was close to the truth. Just before he began a sort of catalog of reasons why the Trumans always had no money, he mentioned the possibility of bad luck. Here he was on solid ground. Ill luck dogged the Trumans. "I have been cutting clover for seed," wrote Farmer Harry. "We have an immense crop of it but it is so short that it is almost impossible to save it." He then turned philosophical. "There is always something the matter with a crop. It's either too dry or too wet or too short or too long or too much or not enough. *If* is the largest word in a farmer's language."[11] Perhaps the Truman farm was, to use the word of Brownie Huber, hoodooed. Years later Truman wrote that the farm had brought bad luck to everyone connected with it, ever since his grandfather died in 1892.[12] John Truman's troubles antedated the farm, but the latter made its own contribution when the road overseer job brought his death after he lifted the boulder in 1914. Grandmother Young's will giving the farm to Uncle Harrison and Martha Ellen Truman led to the family lawsuit. Harry Truman failed every time he tried to impress Bess's mother, Mrs. Wallace. Farm raffles, Texas land, lead and zinc, oil—all failed.

To be sure, bad luck has nothing to do with farming ability.

The second question about Truman, of much more importance than his accomplishments as a farmer, is What qualities did he take from the farm into the presidency? Those qualities affected the government of the United States at a crucial point in its history: the end of World War II and beginning of the cold war. The years of his presidency were surely equal in importance to the era of his predecessor, Franklin D. Roosevelt. His successors for forty years built on the policies Roosevelt and he established. Truman spent the most impressionable years of his life on the farm, as a youngster taking his bearings, so to speak, and then in his twenties and early thirties, when mind and character if not being formed were being hardened. What did the farm do for his presidency?

On this score there is no lack of testimony, and like the comments about his farming there can be no doubt that the special pleaders and hagiographers have been at work. The presidency skews judgments; history disappears in favor of worshipful analyses; people lose sight and move their judgments into the areas of wishes and dreams. There was a time when that favorite American habitat, and if not the American residence of necessity—the log cabin—conferred virtue on a statesman. Farmers have now so diminished in numbers that their heritage, such as it was, no longer seems important to a generation born and bred in the city, accustomed to city sounds and smells and conveniences, and enamored of city virtues. But until fairly recent times, the farm too has been a requirement for the presidency. Truman's farm connections inspired all sorts of imaginings about what the farm did to him, for him, for the nation he eventually headed.

Any theorizing about the farm is bound to hold error, to represent the eye of the beholder. But something of the farm was in the thirty-third president, beyond question. He himself believed the farm the foundation of his life. It is only necessary to mention Truman's undoubted possession of that remarkable quality of mind known as common sense. To define common sense acceptably is impossible. It is a trait the owner possesses in comparison with someone else. But if one sees it as the ability to reduce issues, to remove obfuscations, Harry Truman had it. People who visited the White House often remarked that he listened to their commentaries and then encapsulated them in a swift judgment of what he could or could not do. Where this trait came from, according to Harry Truman's mother, was obvious. "It was on the farm that Harry got his common sense," she said. "He didn't get it in town."

Applied to problems, common sense is the best solvent. While Truman was vice president and presiding over the Senate early in 1945, listening to windy debates that resolved nothing, the soon-to-be president wrote that as he rode behind the farm teams he "settled all the ills of mankind in one way and another."[13] The environment for solution was uncomplicated and simple, and it lacked dignity. The teams went in straight lines, their operations were undisturbingly simple, and the monotonous stretches of Missouri farm land hardly encouraged dignity.

A second quality Truman took from the farm was ability to work. He did just that on the farm, partly because he had to, but also one suspects because he liked to. His life, as one traces it from school days, was filled with doing things, which may have made him feel good or gave him a sense of achievement, which is the same thing. The letters to Bess are full of days spent in rigorous hard work, after which he went to Independence on the train and streetcar or, later, in the Stafford, and sought to get ahead with his girl in the same way.

Ability to work reached over eventually to the White House, and observers noticed how he could turn out paperwork, efficiently and without any feeling that afterward he had to rest. He took afternoon naps, for otherwise he could not stay up until midnight or later, going to functions or reading papers from the briefcase he took home. It was said of him that he played a great deal of poker and that this subtracted from work. He enjoyed poker, which he described as a study in probabilities. But he was never more than a fair player, and the reason was that he worked too hard at his job of being president to spend time on his poker game.

Another probable result of the farm years was the desire to see people.[14] He enjoyed people. On the farm it was so difficult to meet them. It is hardly necessary to add that this liking for people, so evident when anyone met him (people never forgot casual encounters when the president said a few words), bore large political results. This was thoroughly evident during the electoral campaign of 1948. Anyone going to hear the whistle-stop train speeches came away with an impression of a man who not merely believed what he said but enjoyed saying it to responsive crowds. The writer John Hersey took his sons down to the station in Connecticut and afterward had the sure feeling that the president was going to be elected; his behavior differed so much from the coldness of New York's Governor Thomas E. Dewey, the man whose name Truman said rhymed with "hooey."

All these qualities—common sense, ability to work, liking people—served the nation during the parlous time when Truman was president. His critics among both Republicans and Democrats were legion. They remarked crudities of speech or, on one occasion, letter writing, probably deriving from the fact that unlike so many of his predecessors (notably the president he followed), he had not attended an ivy league college where he might have acquired a veneer to protect himself from such errors. The glossy Franklin Roosevelt did not make the remarks Truman offered in public, but FDR was capable of barnyard speech in private and unlike Truman never had seen a barnyard. Apart from small lapses, Truman made only a few serious mistakes as president, most of them connected with the Korean War (failure to ask for a declaration of war at the outset when he could have gotten one, to put on price controls in the beginning of the war, and to prevent General Douglas MacArthur from sending troops across the thirty-eighth parallel). On almost all the large issues, as Speaker Sam Rayburn said, he was right (Sam, a good Democrat, said he was right on *all* the large issues).

A final observation about Truman and the farm. Some people noticed that when he came into the presidency he was a far different individual not only from his immediate predecessor but also from other presidents they could remember. Actually he differed from all the presidents since the beginning of the republic. The third president, Thomas Jefferson, had advanced a maxim of American life that the farm created special virtues in the farmer. Those who labored in the earth, Jefferson wrote, were the chosen people of God, if ever He had a chosen people.[15] One might have thought that many presidents would have come from the farm, or when they anticipated the nation's highest office would have seen to it that they came from the farm.[16] But among Truman's predecessors the only ones who had any acquaintance with the farm were George Washington, Thomas Jefferson, and Ulysses S. Grant. The former were gentleman farmers, the latter a farmer for only three years. Truman was the only real farmer.

Notes

Unless otherwise indicated all oral histories, files, and other special materials cited below are from the Harry S. Truman Library, Independence, Missouri.

Notes to Chapter 1

1. James C. Malin, *The Grassland of North America: Prolegomena to Its History* (Lawrence, Kans., 1947), pp. 169–172; and the same author's *Confounded Rot About Napoleon: Reflections upon Science and Technology, Nationalism, World Depression of the Eighteen-Nineties, and Afterwards* (Lawrence, Kans., 1961), pp. 23–24; Howard B. Schonberger, *Transportation to the Seaboard: The "Communications Revolution" and American Foreign Policy, 1860–1900* (Westport, Conn., 1971) stresses internal transportation.

2. In later years Harry Truman was sensitive to the fact that his father was a mule trader. In the pages of a child's life of the president by Cornelia Spencer, *Straight Furrow: The Biography of Harry S. Truman for Young People* (New York, 1949), pp. 3, 6, he wrote, "Mules only incidental. Cattle, hogs, sheep, horses, and mules. . . . Didn't buy or sell one once in a blue moon." The annotated book is in the Truman Library.

3. Reprinted in *Truman–Prairie Country Visitor*, Spring–Summer, 1986. It is easy to make fun of small-town life, and Lewis E. Atherton pointed out that Main Street did not destroy creative impulses—despite the caricatures by Edgar Lee Masters, Sinclair Lewis, and Thorstein Veblen. See his *Main Street on the Middle Border* (Bloomington, Ind., 1954).

4. The average size of a Missouri farm in 1880 was 129

acres; it was the same ten years later, dropped to 119 in 1900, in 1910 it was 125, in 1920 it was 132, and in 1969 it was 237. *Historical Statistics of the United States: Colonial Times to 1970* (2 vols. (Washington, 1975), vol. I, 461.

5. Robert H. Ferrell, ed., *The Autobiography of Harry S. Truman* (Boulder, Colo., 1980), p. 6.

6. Interview with Mary Jane Truman in *Kansas City Times*, June 14, 1971. Also Harry S. Truman, *Memoirs* 2 vols. (Garden City, N.Y., 1955–56), vol. I, *Year of Decisions*, p. 132.

7. *Autobiography*, p. 6.

8. Uncle Harrison loved to tell stories, perhaps because they subtracted from time he had to work on the farm, and his nephew never forgot them. "On one occasion when I was on the farm the big white field corn was just right for making corn pudding and roasting ears. I told the uncle I was going to the field and get an armful of green corn so we could have a corn pudding. The cook knew how to make an excellent one. When I started out Uncle Harrison was sitting in the yard under an old pine tree and he asked me where I was going. I told him and he asked me if I knew what was the record number of ears of corn a man had eaten at one sitting. Of course I didn't and he proceeded to tell me about a pal of his who had made the record on a bet by eating thirteen roasting ears. This pal cultivated a severe stomachache and had to send for the doctor. The doctor worked over him most of the night and then told him he'd better send for the preacher and do a little praying because medical aid was at an end.

"Well the man was in such pain he finally sent for the parson and the good man prayed for him; he was very earnestly told that he'd have to pray for himself. He told the preacher that he was not a praying man and didn't think he could do it. However the extremity was so great that he finally decided to make the attempt.

"So he got down on his knees in the old-fashioned revival manner and this was his petition to the Almighty:

"'Oh Lord, I am in great pain and misery. I have eaten thirteen roasting ears and I don't seem to be able to take care of them. I am praying to you for help, and Lord I'm not like the damned howling church members in the amen corner; if you'll relieve me of seven of these damned ears of corn I'll try to wrastle around the other six.'" *Autobiography,* pp. 3–5.

9. Labor Day address at the Allegheny County Free Fair in Pittsburgh, September 5, 1949, *Public Papers of the Presidents of the United States: Harry S. Truman, 1949* (Washington, D.C., 1964), p. 460.

10. Margaret Truman, *Harry S. Truman* (New York, 1973), pp. 46–47.

11. *Kansas City Times,* June 14, 1971.

12. For more about Grandmother Young, see below. Mary Martha (Aunt Mat) was born in 1860 and died in 1900. She spent her years with relatives or lived in rooming houses while teaching in country schools. A slight woman, weighing less than one hundred pounds, she suffered from a series of maladies, for which medical knowledge of the time offered no sure remedies. During a trip to Colorado Springs in 1897, she felt ill despite the surroundings of the town that often attracted convalescents; she went to a local physician who put her on a stomach pump (which made her feel worse) and suggested she was suffering from some illness involving the liver. A photograph of Aunt Mat that survived shows an attractive young woman. Spinsterhood bothered her, although she could do little to resolve that problem; she lived in isolated localities and never met suitable young men. One has the impression of a very good person, blighted by the times. A few letters and two diaries display the narrowness of her life. She was easily entertained. She attended church

each Sunday and loved the music and frequently the sermons. On the few trips she made she beheld the sights with enthusiasm. She attended the Chicago World's Fair in 1893 and visited every exhibit. In her diary of that visit is a single mention of her nephew, an entry for June 19: When she returned to her lodging house one evening, "there was an old Italian playing the hand organ, I listened to him a little while and wrote a letter to Harry Truman and that is all." Nancy E. Hendershot, "Mattie Truman: Portrait of a Woman," senior essay, Indiana University department of history, 1987.

13. To Philip B. Perlman, December 22, 1951, William Hillman, ed., *Mr. President* (New York, 1952), p. 236; *Memoirs: Year of Decisions*, p. 15.

14. Margaret Truman, *Harry S. Truman*, p. 50. Some writers, including Cornelia Spencer, asserted that the elder Truman was called "Peanuts." "He was never called this in his life," wrote the irate son. "No one ever heard of it until a muckraker talked to one of the outstanding liars of Independence." Annotation to *Straight Furrow*, p. 6.

15. Mize Peters oral history by J. R. Fuchs, August 8, 21, 1963, March 3, 1964.

16. Stephen S. Slaughter oral history by Niel M. Johnson, April 19, 1984. The interviewer asked Slaughter, son of a Truman neighbor, if John Truman was going to slaughter a Slaughter. "No. Oh no," was the response, "it didn't involve us at all" (p. 105).

17. For the railroad switch, see Bela Kornitzer, "The Story of Truman and His Father," *Parents' Magazine*, March 1951; Kornitzer interviewed Burrus in Independence. A free-lancer, he may have been confused, as he apparently was about other matters. Vivian wrote him a letter of protest and complained to his brother the president that Kornitzer had badly misquoted several people, among them Ethel and Nellie Noland. Letter of

December 8, 1949, "Truman, J. Vivian (folder 2)," box 332, President's Secretary's Files. The president's cryptic response was he had not heard the switch story.

18. Margaret Truman, *Harry S. Truman,* p. 48.

19. Mary Ethel Noland, "Nancy Tyler Holmes' Motto Fitting," *Jackson County Historical Society Journal,* Fall 1967.

20. "Sister Truman was a prominent [church] member and very pious. On her death bed she called her children one at a time and talked to them of the great importance of a preparation for death. . . . Sister Truman before her death said some people thought it was hard to die, but she did not think so." Church report, May 1879, Vertical File.

21. Mary Ethel Noland oral history by J. R. Fuchs, August–September 1965, p. 2; Jonathan Daniels, *The Man of Independence* (Philadelphia, 1950), p. 45.

22. Vivian Truman interview with Jonathan Daniels, September 23, 1949, box 1, Daniels MSS. The trip that took so long must have been between 1854 and 1857 (below, n. 24).

23. A record has survived of one of Solomon Young's entries into Salt Lake City, perhaps not the wagon train carrying the consignment, from the *Deseret News* of August 15, 1860: "A train of some forty wagons, propelled by one hundred and thirty yoke of oxen, arrived on Thursday last, about the same time that Capt. Walling's company came in, belonging to Mr. Solomon Young of Jackson, Mo., and freighted with merchandize for Mr. Ranzhoff.

"The wagons were coupled together in pairs, one behind the other, each pair having on board about sixty hundred pounds and drawn by six pairs of oxen—the usual number attached to those large cumbrous heavy wagons that have been much used in freighting merchandize and Government stores across the plains.

"Mr. Young is of the opinion that the coupling of two wagons together in that manner is the most economical way of freighting to this Territory, as the same amount of freight can be hauled more easily on two light wagons than one of those heavy concerns, heretofore used for freighting purposes, and by hitching them together the expense of teamsters is lessened one half. Light wagons are unquestionably better than heavy ones for such service, but we are not so sure that there can be any thing saved, all things considered, by the coupling operation.

"Mr. Young's cattle look remarkably well and, as we are informed, he did not loose a single ox by accident or otherwise during the trip." Document no. 622, box 22, Miscellaneous Historical Documents.

24. Jonathan Daniels doubted the story of Solomon Young's owning the site of Sacramento, for according to a later history of Jackson County, probably approved by Young, the grandfather did not arrive there until 1855: "In the spring of 1854 he started to California with 1,500 head of cattle, arriving in June, 1855, having lost five hundred on the way. He was engaged in stock-raising there until 1857, when he returned to this county, and has since been in business." *The History of Jackson County Missouri: Containing a History of the County, its Cities, Towns, Etc.* (Kansas City, Mo., 1881), p. 987. Moreover, Sacramento was laid out in 1848—it was in the vast estate of John A. Sutter, who obtained his first grant in 1841 and another in 1845. Daniels to Truman, January 16, 1950, "Daniels, Jonathan," box 98, President's Secretary's Files. The president told Daniels that Grandfather Young's partner in California was named Irvin or Irving and that title to the land may have been in the name of the partnership of Irving and Young. Truman to Daniels, February 2, 1951, "Daniels, Jonathan," box 309, President's Secretary's Files. In another letter of February 27 the president said the

partner cost his grandfather $150,000 in cash. "That was the reason my grandfather had to sell his ranch in California." Truman thought it possible that the grandfather's estate files in Jackson County might have a record, "because when the old man's papers were searched after his death an immense number of unpaid notes were discovered among those papers. There might be something about the California property there because the reason for his disposal of that California ranch was to pay the bankrupt debts . . ." His mother always thought the ranch included part of the site of Sacramento. Letter of January 19, 1950, "Daniels, Jonathan," box 98, President's Secretary's Files.

25. Harry S. Truman interview with Daniels, November 12, 1949, box 1, Daniels MSS.

Notes to Chapter 2

1. Truman may have lived in Clinton and gone to the Young farm from there. He so told his presidential and postpresidential secretary, Rose A. Conway, years later. J. R. Fuchs to Frank Mitchell, February 25, 1966, document no. 30, box 2, Miscellaneous Historical Documents. But see an earlier explanation: "Family moved to the farm in 1905 and I worked another year in the bank to get the piano paid for and a few dollars ahead to pay on a team of horses and then I cut loose and went to the farm." "My Impressions of the Senate, the House, Washington, etc.," undated, "Biographical material," box 168, Senatorial File.

2. "My Impressions of the Senate, the House, Washington, etc.," undated, "Biographical material," box 168, Senatorial File.

3. John J. Strode oral history by Niel M. Johnson, November 18, 1980, p. 50.

4. The forties, however, were not within a single section.

5. Truman to Bess Wallace, September 2, 1911, in Robert H. Ferrell, ed., *Dear Bess: The Letters from Harry to Bess Truman, 1910–1959* (New York, 1983), p. 44.

6. Truman memorandum to Edward Neild, November 20, 1950, "Museum for President Harry S. Truman," box 2, Records of Neild-Somdal Associates relating to Harry S. Truman Library; conversation of Mary Jane Truman with Benedict K. Zobrist and Milton Perry, May 25, 1973, document no. 189, box 6, Miscellaneous Historical Documents; Vivian Truman interview, September 24, 1949, box 1, Daniels MSS. As a child Truman not merely had a racetrack on the north porch but a swing in the front hallway for rainy days and a big one in the yard for good days. *Memoirs: Year of Decisions*, p. 114.

7. Roderick Turnbull, "Truman, Ex-Missouri Farmer," *Farm Journal*, supplement entitled "Farmer's Wife," June 1945. Mary Jane apparently supplied this information.

8. Stephen S. Slaughter oral history, p. 1. He spoke of listening to the sound of the coyotes that had their dens in the Trumans' back pasture. The animals must have been wolves. An item in the *Kansas City Star*, April 1, 1910, reprinted in the paper forty years later, related that "J. Vivian Truman, a farmer near Grandview, unearthed a den of wolves and eight cubs. The old wolves escaped but Mr. Truman captured the cubs and collected $16 bounty from the county court." Clipping enclosed in Vivian to Harry Truman, April 7, 1950, "Truman, J. Vivian (folder 2)," box 332, President's Secretary's Files. Vivian told his brother it was not the litter of wolves raised in the barn cellar. In a letter of April 11, the president responded: "I remember the wolves incident referred to in the article in the paper and I know that that incident is not the one where we raised the wolves in the barn cellar. I think we eventually had to kill all of them because they killed so many chickens."

9. For examples of what research in farming can turn up, see the books by Allan G. Bogue, *Money at Interest: The Farm Mortgage on the Middle Border* (Ithaca, 1955) and *From Prairie to Corn Belt: Farming on the Illinois and Iowa Prairies in the Nineteenth Century* (Chicago, 1963). Through use of scattered but highly informative records the author reconstructs conditions on the farm in "the old days."

10. This and other autobiographical accounts appear in the *Autobiography,* cited in Chapter 1. Description of plowing is on p. 30. At the turn of the century, plowing took a long time. "Now you can get on a tractor and plow night and day—you don't have to feed it or water it—you can get off it whenever you please, take a nap, come back and run it again. I didn't live on the farm in this age. I'm sorry I didn't. I don't want to turn the clock back. I don't want to go back to the horse and buggy age, although some of our Republican friends do." Speech at Dexter, Iowa, September 18, 1948, *Public Papers: Harry S. Truman, 1948* (Washington, 1964), p. 499.

11. Soybeans did not figure in Middle Western agriculture during Truman's time. Until 1919 most soybean production was in the South. In 1909 only 1,629 acres were in soybeans in the entire United States. Thereafter the figure rose rapidly, and there were 9 million by 1939, 15 million by 1950. By the latter dates it was possible to describe Iowa, Missouri, Illinois, Indiana, Ohio, also southern Minnesota and eastern Nebraska, taken together, as not merely "the richest farm on earth" but "The Corn-Soy Belt: Feedbag of Democracy," as in Chapter 7 (pp. 140–161) of Ladd Haystead and Gilbert C. Fite, *The Agricultural Regions of the United States* (Norman, Okla., 1955). Figures for soybean production are on p. 150.

12. Harry to Bess, April 2, 1913, *Dear Bess*, pp. 120–121. For the twelve-disc drill, see speech of February 17, 1959,

"Invitations Massman-Rockhurst," box 81, Invitations File, Postpresidential Files. Harry Truman, farmer, made a distinction between sowing and planting. The threshing machine operator, Leslie C. Hall, inquired if he were planting wheat. "You know," he wrote Bess, "a town farmer always gets his verbs mixed. We sow wheat, oats, and grass seed and plant corn and potatoes. See the difference?" Letter of March 19, 1911, *Dear Bess*, p. 25.

13. "Never said it. She said Harry can lay out as straight a corn row etc." Annotation in Cornelia Spencer, *Straight Furrow*, p. 28. The Spencer book offended the president because of its very title. See also Jonathan Daniels, *Man of Independence*, p. 76. The corn rows did not always come out the way Truman wanted them. "I have to drive the planter because I have a reputation for making straight rows," he wrote to Bess on May 8, 1912. "This year I have succeeded in making a rainbow effect that is very charming to anyone not acquainted with farm work." "From Harry S. Truman to Bess Wallace, May, 1912," box 1, Family Correspondence File, Family, Business and Personal Affairs File.

14. Letter of July 1, *Dear Bess*, p. 88. For the cradling, see letter to Vivian, July 22, 1950, "Truman, J. Vivian (folder 2)," box 332, President's Secretary's Files.

15. The following story is an annotation, in Truman's hand, to Frank McNaughton and Walter Hehmeyer, *This Man Truman* (New York, 1945), pp. 26ff.

16. Letter of July 22, 1912, *Dear Bess*, p. 90. One time a "bonehead" dropped his pitchfork into the mouth of the machine. Undated letter, July 1914, ibid., p. 169.

17. Harry to Bess, October 1, 1911, September 2, 1913, ibid., pp. 50, 136.

18. Letter of January 30, 1912, ibid., p. 70.

19. Letter of June 24, 1912, ibid., p. 87.

20. Letter of August 12, 1912, ibid., pp. 92–93. He

returned home—the railroad went through the Truman farm—and had just put on clean overalls and a soft white shirt, enjoyed supper, and was ready to go upstairs and write a letter to Bess, when his father came in and said that lightning was playing all around and the two of them should go over to a haystack three-quarters of a mile distant where a hay baler had been at work and cover up the hay. This meant walking across a stubble field with low shoes and silk stockings at 9:00 p.m. He went and handed up thirty-two boards a foot wide and fourteen feet long, which his father placed on the hay. Afterward he was certain it would not rain, and it did not; but he thought it would have, had he refused to go.

21. Bill Renshaw, "President Truman: His Missouri Neighbors Tell of His Farm Years," *Prairie Farmer*, May 12, 1945, p. 5.

22. Speech of February 17, 1959; also *Autobiography*, pp. 30–32.

23. *Autobiography*, p. 32.

24. It must have been Boonie who on one occasion got into trouble with his wife. The Trumans had paid him $15 on a Saturday night, and he said he was going to pay some bills, but

I guess he must have hit a crap game first because he didn't get home until Sunday morning. He came up here about noon looking rather dilapidated and said his wife had given him a round with the poker. Said he guessed he'd have to leave as it looked as if he wasn't going to be able to stay home. I guess they must have patched things up because he hasn't said anything more about leaving. He's a great big man, and his wife won't weigh over a hundred pounds. I'm going to work your mother's system and pay on Monday after this. I wouldn't have this fellow leave for anything. He's the best man we ever had. Mamma is of the opinion that he needed braining, but there is always a bond of sympathy between women when a man has been shooting craps and every good man has his failings. I mean good hired men. (Letter of March 24, 1914, *Dear Bess*, pp. 162–163)

25. Truman interview, October 21, 1959, folder 2, box 2, "Mr. Citizen" File. The average pay per day for a hired man, without board and room, fluctuated between $1.35 and $1.40 from 1910 through 1915; in 1916 it was $1.50 and in 1917 it rose to $1.90 (*Historical Statistics of the United States: Colonial Times to 1970*, vol. I, 468).

26. Nationally, the numbers of tractors rose rapidly from 1910, when there were 1,000, until 1920, when there were 246,000. But the big rise came later. By 1940 the nation's farmers were using 1.5 million; by 1950, 2.5 million. The disappearance of horses and mules may well have been a prominent factor in the Great Depression of the 1930s. Sixteen million horses disappeared in that decade alone, most of them to soap factories. A single horse ate fifty bushels of oats and two tons of hay each year. In 1910, 72 million out of 325 million acres of cropland fed farm horses and mules, and another 16 million fed nonfarm horses—that is, over one-fourth of crop acres. In 1943 the figure was 14 million out of 349 million. Farmers diverted this acreage to dairy production, pigs, and other farm products that materially affected the farm surplus problem. They meanwhile became customers of the petroleum industry. *Historical Statistics of the United States: Colonial Times to 1970*, vol. I, 469; A. N. Johnson, "The Impact of Farm Machinery on the Farm Economy," *Agricultural History*, vol. 24 (1950), 59; William L. Cavert, "The Technological Revolution in Agriculture, 1910–1955," ibid., vol. 30 (1956), 19–20; Richard S. Kirkendall, "Harry S. Truman: A Missouri Farmer in the Golden Age," ibid., vol. 48 (1974), 476.

27. Truman interview, October 21, 1959. For many years

Missouri was the largest mule-holding state in the nation until displaced by Texas in 1900. That year Missouri still had 238,519 mules, and in 1910—with Texas continuing in the lead—342,700. Its mules were only about one-fourth of the state's mule and horse population. The Missouri ratio of mules to horses was of course higher than that of the nation, which in 1906 was 3 million mules to 18 million horses. *Historical Statistics of the United States: Colonial Times to 1970*, vol. I, 519. By nature a mule was less spirited than a horse, but wiser. Stubbornness, if such it was, derived from that fact. A mule responded to kind treatment and performed more work under steady exhortation than by being beaten. A mule perhaps even liked the rhythmic cadence of profanity. Being a hybrid, it was a stronger biological specimen—more resistant to disease, longer lived—than a horse. The average working life of a mule was eighteen years, a horse fifteen. G. K. Renner, "The Mule in Missouri Agriculture," *Missouri Historical Review*, vol. 73 (1979–80), 442–443, 446, 448. See also "Mules Were Best on RFD Routes, You Couldn't Reason with an Automobile," ibid., vol. 46 (1951–52), 205, reprinting a letter from the Macon, Missouri, postmaster, from *The Fairfax Forum*. According to this letter of 1903, "A Missouri mule will go where no automobile in the land would dare to tread. . . . Nothing will discourage him. We use 'em on all of our routes, and I know. . . . A mule eats more than an automobile but he gives greater results."

28. Letter of November 28, 1911, *Dear Bess*, p. 61.

29. John D. Hicks, "The Western Middle West, 1900–1914," *Agricultural History*, vol. 20 (1946), 67.

30. Letters of March 23, and June 24, 1912, *Dear Bess*, pp. 79, 87.

31. Letter of January 12, 1914, ibid., p. 155. "Doc" Young, the veterinarian, once haggled with Truman over a cow, the difference between $75 and $80, and when it became a

matter of Harry's dinner—Mary Jane telling him at 1:00 p.m. that they were going to put the food away—the vet gave in. "I wanted that cow," Young said, "so I said, 'Harry, I don't want to see you starve to death over a matter of $5. I'll pay $80 for that cow.'" Edward R. Schauffler, *Harry Truman: Son of the Soil* (Kansas City, 1945), p. 34.

32. Letter of December 30, 1913, *Dear Bess*, p. 151.

33. Letter of May 9, 1911, ibid., p. 32.

34. Edward R. Schauffler, *Harry Truman*, p. 35.

35. Samuel R. Guard, "From Plowboy to President," *Breeder's Gazette*, June, 1945, pp. 5–6; Wayne C. Neely, "President Harry S. Truman: Shorthorn Breeder," *Shorthorn Country*, vol. 2 (1975), 36–38; Edward R. Schauffler, *Harry Truman*, p. 37.

36. Letter marked "April Fool's Day," 1915, *Dear Bess*, p. 80.

37. Letter of December 9, 1913, ibid., p. 149.

38. Letters of September 17, 30, 1912, ibid., pp. 97, 99.

39. Letter of September 9, 1912, ibid., p. 96.

40. Ole H. V. Stalheim, "The Hog Cholera Battle and Veterinary Professionalism," *Agricultural History*, vol. 62 (1988), 116–121; also William L. Cavert, "The Technological Revolution in Agriculture, 1910–1955."

41. The following is from a letter of December 15, 1913, *Dear Bess*, pp. 149–150.

42. Edward R. Schauffler, *Harry Truman*, p. 37.

43. Letters of May 3, 9, 1911, *Dear Bess*, pp. 31–33.

Notes to Chapter 3

1. The commission's chairman, Bailey, was the expert member, even beyond the experiences of the editor of *Wallaces' Farmer*. The latest scholarly account of the renowned Cornell agriculturist is by Margaret Beattie Bogue, "Liberty Hyde Bailey, Jr. and the Bailey Family

Farm," *Agricultural History*, vol. 36, no. 1 (Winter 1989), 26–48.

2. 60th Cong., 2d sess., Senate doc. 705, *Report of the Country Life Commission* (Washington, 1909), p. 17. Roosevelt's comment in the letter of transmittal is on p. 5. Truman made a derogatory reference in a letter to Bess on January 26, 1911 (*Dear Bess*, p. 21): "You know our friend Roosevelt appointed a country life commission to spend the extra cash in the U.S. Treasury." Actually the president had asked Congress for $25,000, and did not get it. For the commission, see Clayton S. Ellsworth, "Theodore Roosevelt's Country Life Commission," *Agricultural History*, vol. 34 (1960), 155–172; William L. Bowers, "Country-Life Reform, 1900–1920: A Neglected Aspect of Progressive Era History," ibid., vol. 45 (1971), 211–221; Olaf F. Larson and Thomas B. Jones, "The Unpublished Data from Roosevelt's Commission on Country Life," ibid., vol. 50 (1976), 583–599.

3. Letter of January 26, 1911, *Dear Bess*, p. 21.

4. C. Warren Ohrvall, "Information on Harry S. Truman's Masonic Career," 1983, Vertical File.

5. Ruby Jane Hall oral history by Niel M. Johnson, December 6, 1980, p. 20. Mary Jane was very active in the Stars and became worthy grand matron of the Missouri O.E.S. in 1950. Ruby Hall may have exaggerated when she said Truman would bid as high as $4 for her box. In a letter of December 2, 1913, he explained that the average price at least at one social was $1.25, the highest $2.25. "Then I got a little six-year-old girl's box. She had expressed the hope that I would and there was nothing for it but to do it." At this social Truman bought three boxes decorated with moons, stars, diamonds, hearts, and other shapes and was so full of cake and pie and flossy sandwiches he thought he never wanted to see any more. *Dear Bess*, p. 148.

6. Letter of November 10, 1913, ibid., p. 142.

7. *Autobiography*, p. 28. In the autobiographical memoir he dated the Union incursion as 1863, but it probably was the Jim Lane raid of 1861. Also, the house was different—the one from which Grandmother Young moved to the big house in 1867 or 1868.

8. Rear platform remarks at Waterloo, Iowa, October 29, 1952, *Public Papers: Harry S. Truman, 1952–53* (Washington, 1966), p. 978. "I heard Mr. Bryan say one time that the first convention he attended was at Philadelphia in 1876, and he crawled in through a window, and that ever since that time they had been trying to put him out over the transom but never had succeeded." Speech at New York City, May 15, 1952, ibid., p. 204.

9. Harry to Bess, March 17, 1914, Family Correspondence File; National Archives to Truman Library, June 13, 1969, Vertical File; *Autobiography*, p. 36.

10. Truman interview, November 12, 1949, box 1, Daniels MSS.

11. Letter of November 28, 1911, *Dear Bess*, p. 62.

12. Letter of December 31, 1910, ibid., p. 18.

13. Gaylon Babcock oral history, p. 21.

14. Myra Colgan, daughter of Aunt Emma, was getting married, and he was practicing the wedding march from *Lohengrin*. Letter of September 17, 1912, *Dear Bess*, pp. 97–98. After the box social he had played. "We had a dance after it was over. I furnished the music and the rest danced. Even Papa got gay and fixed up an old-fashioned square dance. Mamma wouldn't go at all. We all told her she'd just about lose the old gentleman if she doesn't watch him closely." Letter of December 2, 1913, ibid., p. 148.

15. Margaret Truman, *Bess W. Truman* (New York, 1986), p. 30.

16. Letter of February 3, 1914, *Dear Bess*, p. 158.

17. Letter of January 26, 1911, ibid., pp. 20–21.

18. Letters of January 12, August 12, 1912, ibid., pp. 68, 92.

19. Letter of May 2, 1912, ibid., pp. 84–85.

20. Letter of September 17, 1912, ibid., p. 97.

21. 1914, undated, ibid., p. 172.

22. 1915, undated, ibid., p. 183.

Notes to Chapter 4

1. Letter of November 10, 1913, *Dear Bess*, p. 143.

2. Letters of May 12, 1912, January 6, and April 2, 1913, ibid., pp. 83, 111, 120.

3. It is possible that Harrison paid his share. Half of $9,500, the money paid the relatives, came to $4,750, and the legal fees totaled $3,000 and half of them was $1,500. Harrison might have calculated that he would pay half of the money owed to the relatives, but none of the fees—that the Trumans, not him, had brought the suit. That then would account for the mortgage of $7,500.

4. Letter of October 22, 1911, *Dear Bess*, pp. 53–54.

5. One letter along this line was prophetic, if tinged with Truman's usual self-deprecation and roundabout proposals of marriage: "How does it feel being engaged to a clodhopper who has ambitions to be Governor of Montana and Chief Executive of U.S. He'll do well if he gets to be a retired farmer. That was sure a good dream though, and I have them in the daytime, even night, along the same line. It looks like an uphill business sometimes though. But I intend to keep peggin' away and I suppose I'll arrive at something. You'll never be sorry if you take me for better or for worse because I'll always try to make it better." Letter of November 10, 1913, ibid., p. 143.

6. Letters of May 4, 12, 1914, ibid., pp. 167–168.

7. Undated, early 1916, ibid., pp. 185–186.

8. Letter of April 27, 1916, ibid., p. 198.

9. Letter of July 25, 1916, ibid., p. 204.

10. Bill Renshaw, "President Truman: His Missouri Neighbors Tell of His Farm Years," p. 19.

11. Truman interview with Jonathan Daniels, July 28, 1949, box 1, Daniels MSS. Truman had told Bess in 1916 that he was "in hock" for "about $11,000" because he had put up all the money (letters of August 5, September 7, *Dear Bess*, pp. 209, 212), but one suspects that Hughes who was an honest man then paid his one-third of the losses,leaving Truman with the balance. By this time Truman owned two-thirds of the mine. Culbertson had deeded his third interest so Truman could obtain a loan from James F. Blair, cashier of the Bank of Belton and his mentor in the Masonic Order. Blair told Truman, "I deserved to lose the whole shebang. Said I deserved a bump for going in with Culbertson. He knows him well. He finally said that if Culbertson assigned me his rights until I got my money back, he'd help. I called Culbertson and he agreed." May 26, ibid., p. 200.

12. "That Teter lease had 320 acres and was on top of a tableland above a beautiful plain. We had it leased and a well down nine hundred feet when the money gave out. A St. Paul outfit wanted fifty per cent of the lease to finish the well but my partners wouldn't agree and I was gone. The lease was forfeited and taken over by another syndicate, a well drilled at the other end of it and from one end to the other that 320 acres never had a dry hole. It was worth about seven million dollars when I got home from the war." "My Impressions . . . ," undated, "Biographical material," box 168, Senatorial File.

13. In National Guard units the men elected officers.

14. *Independence Examiner*, reprinted October 4, 1964, Vertical File.

15. D. Jerome Tweton, "The Golden Age of Agriculture,

1897–1917," *North Dakota History*, vol. 37 (1970), 46; John D. Hicks, "The Western Middle West, 1900–1914," p. 72.

16. John D. Hicks, "The Western Middle West, 1900–1914," p. 72.

17. Ibid., p. 73; Peter H. Lindert, "Long-run Trends in American Farmland Values," *Agricultural History*, vol. 62, no. 3 (Summer 1988), 48; John Meador oral history by Niel M. Johnson, November 18, 1980, pp. 1–3; Thomas J. Pressly and William H. Scofield, eds., *Farm Real Estate Values in the United States by Counties: 1850–1959* (Seattle, 1965), p. 36; Harry to Bess, March 24, 1914, *Dear Bess*, p. 162.

18. For the percentage increase between 1900 and 1910, above, and for figures in the next two paragraphs, including data regarding the nominal prices for acreage with 1960 New England consumer dollars, I am indebted to the excellent article by Lindert cited in the preceding note, especially pp. 47–55. Through the kindness of its author I was able to see his much larger unpublished essay of the same name (no. 45 [February 1988]) in the working paper series of the Agricultural History Center, University of California at Davis. Lindert shows conclusively the error of the classical British economists, Malthus and Ricardo, who believed that pressure of population increases the value of land. These theoreticians took the obvious fact that it is more difficult to increase land than people or capital goods and other productive inputs and made a theory out of it. John Stuart Mill, Henry George, and Alfred Marshall all agreed that land values had to rise (Lindert impishly writes that George and Marshall agreed on little else). Still, as he relates in his article and the working paper, if one measures nominal land prices against a proper benchmark, his choice being 1960 New England consumer dollars, the theory breaks down.

19. Land in Jackson County went up until 1920, when it reached $229 per acre, then dropped a bit, rose toward

the 1920 figure, and tumbled: 1925, $185; 1930, $211; 1935, $125; 1940, $112. Thomas J. Pressly and William E. Scofield, eds., *Farm Real Estate Values*.

20. For Peek the parity period was those years, save for tobacco, which was from 1919 to 1929. He was an evangelist for the farmers and singlemindedly pushed his point of parity. Had he shown more understanding of larger issues—how, say, rewarding farmers might have affected other parts of the economy—he might have been more successful. See the excellent account by Gilbert C. Fite, *George N. Peek and the Fight for Farm Parity* (Norman, Okla., 1954).

21. The height of farm population, 32 million, came between 1910 and 1917, save for the recession period of 1921–1922, and worst of the Great Depression, 1933–1935, when it again rose to its 1910–1917 figure. Thereupon a rapid decline set in. *Historical Statistics of the United States: Colonial Times to 1970*, vol. I, 457.

22. Abstract of January 25, 1950, "1967," box 1, Arthur Mag MSS.

23. Memorandum by J. R. Fuchs, September 7, 1965, Vertical File.

24. Truman's calculation appears in a memorandum in the Vertical File.

25. For calculations of the county's loss I am indebted to John K. Hulston, Ralph E. Hunt, and Nicolas Spulber. The price deflator is in *Bureau of Labor Statistics Handbook*, bulletin 2340 (August 1989), p. 475, table 113. Truman wrote out in longhand the calculation remarked above in note 24, but did not break down the county's income from crops nor expenses from maintenance; an exact calculation would require breakdown and deflation by date. No taxes were paid on the farm from 1938 to 1940, and the property was off the rolls from 1940 to 1945; unpaid taxes should be included in the county's loss.

26. *Kansas City Star,* January 27, 1958.
27. Interview of October 21, 1959. "I can't help but wish," he added, "that I could have kept that farm as it was in the beginning."
28. *Kansas City Times,* November 7, 1966.
29. For the exactitude with which work was done, see Robert T. Bray, *Archaeological Survey and Testing at the Truman Farm Home and Grounds, Grandview, Missouri* (Kansas City, Mo., 1983). Initial attendance was disappointing—2,800 visitors per year, seven or eight daily, compared to 100,000 annually to the Truman house in Independence. *Kansas City Times,* May 13, 1989.

Notes to Chapter 5

1. B. F. Ervin, Sr., "He was a Good Man with a Pitchfork, Too," *Kansas City Times,* July 10, 1963.
2. Letter of February 27, 1912, *Dear Bess,* p. 75; interview of July 28, 1949, box 1, Daniels MSS; Margaret Truman, *Harry S. Truman,* pp. 48–49.
3. Stephen S. Slaughter oral history, p. 34.
4. Gaylon Babcock oral history, p. 13.
5. Letter of August 5, 1916, *Dear Bess,* p. 209.
6. Stephen Slaughter oral history, pp. 34ff.
7. Ibid., p. 35. "I remember the Sunday afternoon Father and Mother drove over to the Truman home to visit him. It was known at the time that Mr. Truman had only a short time to live. And I remember the sadness Father and Mother felt after the visit. The four had had a long talk together and it was much on Mr. Truman's mind that as a business man he had not been a success. He looked on his life as a failure. Father had given him what comfort he could: the fine neighbor he had always been, the friends he had made, the useful work he had performed, the unstinting effort he had given to every undertaking, the

fine family he had reared. Looking back on it now, the great irony of it all—the father of a future President of the United States believing his life had been a failure." Stephen S. Slaughter, *History of a Missouri Farm Family: The O. V. Slaughters, 1700–1944* (Harrison, N.Y., 1978), p. 71.

8. For some years the Trumans evidently used the barn cistern in an inefficient way, employing pails to fill troughs for the stock. At last Harry Truman set out to solve the problem and found the cistern under direct control of His Majesty. "Today has been the most satanic we've had, to my notion," he wrote.

I took an energetic spell last week and decided to clean out the barn cistern and put a pump on it. Well, last Friday evening Boon and I began draining water about four o'clock I guess. Well, we took bucket-about until after six. I guess we must have taken out some hundreds of gallons—and it looked as if there was as much water as ever. We finally quit because it got dark. I took it on myself to finish getting the water out of the cistern by this afternoon. I'll bet I drew some two hundred gallons more or less, and there is still some water in the blooming thing. I'll get its goat tomorrow though. Then I want it to rain about three inches and fill the thing up. I was on the east side of the barn where breezes were scarce and sunshine was plentiful and exceeding hot, as Moses has remarked about the future residence of some of us. (Letter of September 9, 1912, *Dear Bess*, pp. 96–97)

The silo issue—why the Trumans never had a silo—may have come out of the following experience:

Talk about a dirty job now. There's one that can give any other job you can think of cards and spades and beat it out for real downright dirt. The man who was feeding the machine had a bandana handkerchief tied right over his face. It didn't even have eye holes in it. He looked like some of Captain Kidd's victims must have looked after that gentleman got through with them. Then the man inside the silo has to walk and walk and then walk some more. It is just the same as being in a jug. You can imagine how very nice that would be on a day like yesterday. I told the fellow inside that I'd dispense with all the clothes I could if I were going to work in it. I hope I'll never have to work in one. (Letter of September 2, 1913, ibid., pp. 135–136)

9. John D. Hicks, "The Western Middle West, 1900–1914," p. 69.

10. The Trumans did obtain a small settlement from the railroad for losing a small piece of land.

11. Harry to Bess, August 22, 1913, *Dear Bess*, p. 134.

12. Letter of October 1, 1940, ibid., p. 447.

13. *Autobiography*, p. 30.

14. Richard S. Kirkendall believes Truman became more gregarious, more sociable and popular on the farm, after being "a very shy, withdrawn person as a child and young adult." "Harry S. Truman: A Missouri Farmer in the Golden Age," p. 483. Truman himself wrote, "I thought of Cincinnatus and a lot of other farm boys who had made good and I thought maybe by cussing mules and plowing corn I could perhaps overcome my shyness and amount to something." "My Impressions . . . ," undated, "Biographical material," box 168, Senatorial File.

15. *Notes on Virginia*, quoted in A. Whitney Griswold, *Farming and Democracy* (New York, 1948), p. 30.

16. A biographer once asked Franklin Roosevelt about his estate, Hyde Park. "It's not an estate," Roosevelt replied, with an expression of annoyance. "It's a farm. . . Must our farm be called an estate merely because I'm governor, or because it's been in the family a long time, or because there are flower gardens there?. . . Call it by its right name—a farm. I don't like estates and I *do* like farms."

151

William Burlie Brown, *The People's Choice: The Presidential Image in the Campaign Biography* (Baton Rouge, 1960), p. 86.

Harry S. Truman's family tree

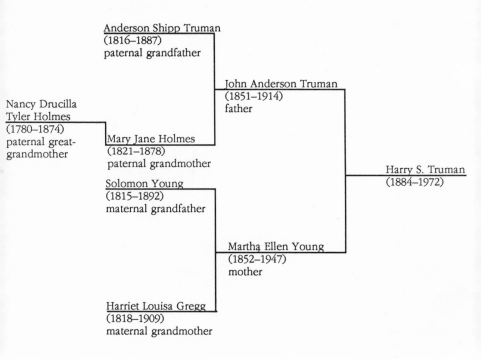

Anderson Shipp Truman
(1816–1887)
paternal grandfather

John Anderson Truman
(1851–1914)
father

Nancy Drucilla
Tyler Holmes
(1780–1874)
paternal great-
grandmother

Mary Jane Holmes
(1821–1878)
paternal grandmother

Harry S. Truman
(1884–1972)

Solomon Young
(1815–1892)
maternal grandfather

Martha Ellen Young
(1852–1947)
mother

Harriet Louisa Gregg
(1818–1909)
maternal grandmother

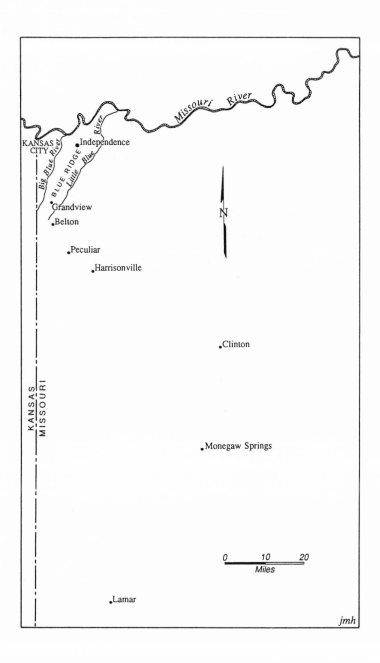

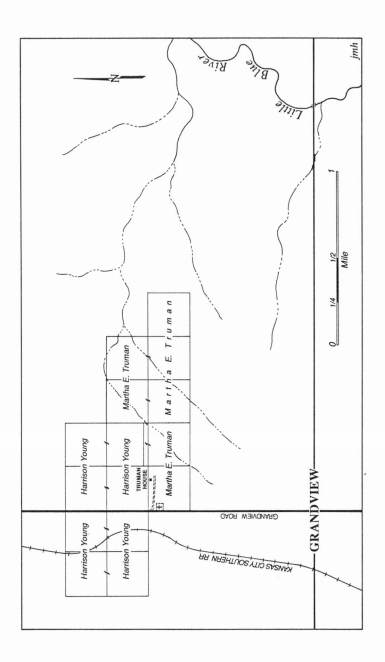

155

Index

Index

159

160